On the Wing

On the Wing

American Poems
of Air *and* Space Flight

Edited by Karen Yelena Olsen

University of Iowa Press, Iowa City

University of Iowa Press, Iowa City 52242

Printed on acid-free paper

Library of Congress Cataloging-in-Publication Data
On the wing: American poems of air and space flight /
edited by Karen Yelena Olsen.
   p.   cm.
Includes bibliographical references and index.
ISBN 0-87745-945-2 (cloth), 0-87745-944-4 (pbk.)
1. Aeronautics—Poetry. 2. Space flight—Poetry.
3. Flight—Poetry. 4. American Poetry. I. Olsen,
Karen Yelena, 1945–.
PS595.A26 O5 2005   2004062052
811′.008/0356 22

05 06 07 08 09 C 5 4 3 2 1
05 06 07 08 09 P 5 4 3 2 1

In memory of Yelena and Art,

and of Lori

We race.   We rise.

We must sing a new song of our speed,

We must chant a new hymn of ascent.

Soon we shall make ourselves lungs

of the sponge of the spaces

And wings

of the plumes of the clouds.

ANONYMOUS

Contents

III. AIRPLANE VISIONS, AIRPORT TRUTHS

VI. SPACE ODYSSEYS

Preface

On the Wing is a book that grew out of a passion for flight and a lifelong love affair with literature. As a poet, teacher of poetry, and amateur pilot, I've long dreamed of compiling an anthology of American air and space poetry.

For years I've sought out poems about airplanes, balloons, spaceships, blimps, pilots, passengers, and airports. Passionately and indiscriminately, I've collected sonnets, limericks, haiku, and epics—polished works and pure doggerel. My search has taken me through yellowed newspapers, dusty library shelves, bookstores, databases, Internet sites, anthologies, and periodicals. Gracious librarians and flight historians have sent me clippings from archives, from the *Congressional Record*, from rare book collections. Friends, students, and total strangers have sent me verse. Over the years the stack of poems has grown alarmingly.

Over the same years I have taught courses in literature, primarily to men and women of the United States Air Force. My students provided a valuable test audience, offering fresh insights into the poems and the world of aviation. I have talked as well with airline crews, jet jockeys, helicopter pilots, crop dusters, and flight instructors. These fellow flyers have generously answered my questions and guided my speculations, sharing with me their own enthusiasms.

This book began, then, as a collection of poems that salute the achievements of aerospace exploration. But over the years it has acquired a higher purpose. As I read and reread, gathered new poems, sifted through earlier discoveries, I gained a new appreciation for the range and depth of the poets' response to events in the air. It is a privilege to present these poems. Through them, *On the Wing* celebrates the lyrical energy and excellence of American poetry in this first century of flight.

Karen Yelena Olsen

On the Wing

Introduction

The year 2003 marked a full century of aviation, one that began when the Wright brothers' fragile craft lifted a few feet off the sand dunes of Kitty Hawk. Only sixty-five years later, the crew of *Apollo 11* landed on the gray dust of the lunar surface, 250,000 miles from Earth. Just as the advent of human flight radically redefined our aspirations and fears, its subsequent evolution has revolutionized our economic, social, and political lives. For poets, the experience of flight has provided a whole new range of images and perspectives, while challenging traditional assumptions about the subject matter and language of poetry. The wide-ranging response of American poets gives us insight into the exploration of air and space as it intersects with the shaping forces of our national experience.

On the Wing gathers together modern works by American poets, reflecting the importance of the United States' contributions to aviation and space exploration. But ever since humans first dreamed of sprouting wings, poets have sought to express what Yeats called the "lonely impulse of delight" that drives us toward the skies.

From ancient times, the idea of flight has carried with it the aura of the divine. The prophet Isaiah promises flight as the reward of the righteous: "They shall mount up with wings as eagles." For Homer and the classical Greeks, wings are reserved for the Olympian gods, who speed effortlessly and instantaneously through the air. When Daedalus and Icarus dare to usurp this divine power, they are swiftly punished for their hubris. But even as Icarus's tragic fate foreshadows our mortality, his ascent toward the sun has come to symbolize the boundless aspirations of humanity.

When the dream of flight at last came true, when humans first floated upward in the hot-air and hydrogen balloons of the eighteenth century, the poets' imagination rose with them. Philip Freneau, watching the first New World balloon ascent in 1793, felt its import for the future:

on silken wings
Beyond our groveling race you rise
And soaring from terrestrial things
Explore a passage to the skies.
("Reflections on Balloons")

Just 110 years later, Orville and Wilbur Wright took off in their engine-powered "flying machine."

As Robert Wohl reminds us in *A Passion for Wings*, the advent of the airplane was for many people "an *aesthetic* event" (1). This is especially true of the poets. From the beginnings of human flight, they have explored its sensory aspects, taking pleasure in the shapes of the aircraft, in the ballet of aerial maneuvers, and in the new vistas of earth, sea, and cloud afforded the airborne observer. Especially in the early years of aviation, both pilots and poets reveled in the physical sensations of open-cockpit flight—the roar of the engine, the smell of hot oil, the wind whipping past, the lift of takeoff, the rush of sheer speed.

Early enthusiasm for flight was not limited to American poets; in Italy the Futurists found in the airplane inspiration for both poetry and art. But the fervid optimism of their response did set them apart from their English peers. In his 1908 novel *The War in the Air*, England's H. G. Wells imagined the aerial destruction of New York City, while Paul Bewsher, in his long poem *The Bombing of Bruges*, described the real-life nightmare of World War I. American writers conjured different visions. As Joseph J. Corn observes in *The Winged Gospel*, when airplanes first appeared in the sky, "Englishmen looked aloft and saw shadows while Americans saw bright harbingers of peace and a new sign in the heavens" (45).

Why the difference in outlook? Geography played a major role: with oceans for its borders, Americans felt secure from airborne peril. But Corn also notes that, like the earlier steamboats and locomotives, airplanes spoke to the deep American faith in machines as agents of social progress. Emily Dickinson and Walt Whitman, for instance, were both fascinated by trains. At the same time, in a country steeped in Christian evangelism, "flight as a technical achievement blurred with deeply embedded associations of the heavens as a place of spiritual promise" (49). Laurence Goldstein adds to this brew of symbolic meanings our "native myth of manifest destiny," in which the airplane is seen as offering Americans "a mobile and beatific vision of a new heaven and a new earth" (*Flying* 4, 6). Thus, many early poems offered utopian visions of a new Air Age bringing peace, social equality, spiritual uplift, and the erasure of national boundaries.

Even the outbreak of World War I did little to dampen American enthusiasm. The public, as Corn says, persisted in seeing "air war as purer than ground war" (11). And since America's role in the war was limited in scope, with no major American poet-pilot returning, like Bewsher, to give a realistic account of wartime flying, poets were free to put a romantic gloss on their imaginings.

Romantic too is the figure of the aviator-hero, an idealized type whose features were soon firmly established. The pilot is seen as a loner who, though loyal to the chivalric brotherhood of fellow aviators, remains aloof from more ordinary mortals. He (very occasionally she) possesses a special genius and a generous, lofty soul. Courageous and daring, free of petty or worldly motives, he is passionately dedicated to his calling. As Wohl remarks, these are traits also ascribed—or self-ascribed—to poets and artists, a gratifying parallel implicit in poetry of the 1920s and '30s, where a recurring image evokes the lone pilot flying off into the clouds (27).

This insistent glorification of the aviator began with the image accorded the Wright brothers and continued with portraits of the World War I "aces," of stunt pilots like Lincoln Beachey, and of aerial explorers like Richard Byrd. It reached its apogee in the thousands of poems written in praise of Charles Lindbergh's 1927 flight from New York to Paris.

Corn reminds us that Lindbergh's solo flight over the Atlantic also tapped into Americans' "mythologized visions of their frontier past," while his modest and clean-cut public image affirmed for them "the continued strength of pioneer instincts and virtues" (25). Not surprisingly, this same figure of the pilot-hero appears later in the century as well, notably in poems of war, in celebrations of America's space exploits, and in elegiac verse generally. And sometimes he is joined or displaced by his mocking postmodern shadow, the antihero.

Other trends in American social history are also manifest in the poems of this anthology. Modern focus on race and gender, for instance, has brought renewed interest in women aviators like Amelia Earhart and Jacqueline Cochran and attention to neglected aspects of aviation history, such as the role of the Tuskegee airmen in World War II.

Meanwhile, advances in aviation technology have led to changes in the way flight is experienced and described. Though many poems throughout the century record the transformation of familiar geography through the lens of aerial perspective, this theme modulates over time as planes with pressurized cabins fly at ever higher altitudes. In midcentury poems, the visionary landscapes and cloudscapes fade, while images of takeoff and landing acquire sharper focus.

At the same time, flying begins to be seen less as an individual experience and more as a social phenomenon. By the 1950s romantic notions of aviation as a means toward democracy and world peace have evaporated. Increasingly, the airplane is recognized as just another means of mass transport. But even if aviation has ceased to thrill the general public, poets continue to find in it new sources of interest. And as aeronautical advances have brought airplanes into the lives of ordinary citizens, more people are writing about flight in all its aspects, bringing new complexities in attitude, approach, and poetic style. More women are writing poems about flight, for example, while poets like Simon Ortiz and Carter Revard situate aviation within the context of Native American experience.

Changing technology has shaped poetry in other ways as well. The latter part of the twentieth century saw the advent of wide-bodied airliners, planes in which most passengers are denied the pleasures of a window seat. With no view to the outside and little or no sensation of motion, airborne poets now take greater interest in the crowded microcosm of the cabin— its routines and programmed distractions, its protocols and hierarchies, its peculiarly modern solitude, its boredom, so often masking fear. Or their thoughts turn inward altogether, and they write poems about preflight goodbyes, postflight expectations. Together with this growing body of "passenger poetry," a related genre has emerged, focusing on the airport and its ambiguous place in our lives.

Wohl points out a more disturbing consequence of increasing flight altitudes, one seen as early as World War I. To escape antiaircraft fire, pilots flew as high as possible, and "the earth became a target as far removed from the personal experience of the observer or the bombardier as a distant planet" (285). Such emotional distance has only intensified in succeeding conflicts, and many poems explore this frightening dehumanization of modern aerial warfare, especially the impersonal havoc wreaked by bomber aircraft. In James Dickey's long poem "The Firebombing," the ex-pilot narrator, remembering a bombing sortie over Japan, exults in "this detachment, the honored aesthetic evil, the greatest sense of power in one's life" (*Poems* 185). The dive-bombing aviators in William Everson's "The Raid" rejoice to see "sweet chaos blossom below."

It was World War II that initiated this new theme in American poetry, the airplane as a weapon of war. In the 1940s an entire generation of American poets was plunged into military service. Many of them served in aircrews, where they witnessed firsthand the thrills and terrors of aerial combat and the devastation of aerial bombardment. Dickey's peers include John Ciardi, Richard Eberhart, Edward Field, Richard Hugo, Randall Jarrell, William Meredith, Howard Nemerov, George Oppen, and Richard Snyder—men for whom wartime aviation supplied both the subject of their youthful poems and a rich source of imagery and reflection for their later work. The same can be said for Vietnam poet-pilots like Walt McDonald.

War poems often dwell on that most dramatic of flight experiences, death in the air. From the beginning, this somber theme punctuates both the history and the poetry of air and space. In the early years, aerial elegies are reserved for the pilot, his solitary end evoking for poets the age-old image of Icarus falling. Later in the century, the astronauts who died in the Apollo and space shuttle disasters are often eulogized in similar terms. But in recent years a grim new genre of elegy has emerged, poems that mourn the multiple deaths incurred when airliners fail to take off, or plummet to the earth, or explode in the sky. The impact of these poems draws on the very personal terror such events spark in both poet and reader. We share an identity as past and future passengers, all too aware of our helpless and vulnerable state.

The history and evolving technology of flight have created not only new poetic genres but also new challenges for poetic language. Early biplanes— visibly fragile objects made of wood and wire and linen fabric—were easy to romanticize. But in the 1920s and '30s, planes begin to look like what they really are: vehicles for transporting payloads, industrial objects produced on assembly lines by corporations whose goal is profit, not adventure. The engineers who design airplanes, like the pilots and navigators who fly them, hold a pragmatic view of aviation and express themselves in decidedly un-poetic prose.

What language then is the poet of flight to use for this ultimate machine dream? According to Wohl, early European poets took one of two ap-proaches: either they attempted "to connect aviation with a known past" by using "the poetic discourse of a pre-industrial age" or else they chose to view it as "the harbinger and agent of a new and fundamentally different machine-driven civilization" (138).

American poets, facing the same dilemma, have made similar choices. Many have opted to naturalize the new technology, wrapping it in the rhetorical traditions of earlier verse—often through allusions to the myths of Icarus and Daedalus or through organic metaphors linking plane and pilot to those natural flyers, the birds.

Other writers, rejecting this neoromantic language, have elected to adopt the relentlessly prosaic language of the practitioners of flight. Goldstein notes that Muriel Rukeyser, like other poets writing in the thirties, used in those days "the plainest of plain styles." But, he argues, such rhetoric proved inadequate to the task: in these poems, "the industrial muse fails to provide satisfactory wings to the poet" (*Flying* 128, 129).

The search has continued for a modern poetic style, "a language of praise both appropriate and dramatic" (*Flying* 124). By midcentury William Carlos Williams could assert that "the serious poet has admitted the whole arma-mentarium of the industrial age to his poems." Robert Vas Dias, who quotes Williams's comment, carries this idea further, stressing modern poets' "use of the mechanistic, 'impersonal' and industrial image to locate the position of contemporary man" (xxxiv). In the verse of Williams, Nemerov, Hall, and others, one can indeed hear a more streamlined muse of the machine age taking wing.

Many of our newest industrial images come from the sphere of space exploration, a realm that has gripped the imagination of nearly every American writer of the past forty-odd years. Poetic responses to each new space exploit reveal an astonishing variety. Reviewing the poems of his 1973 collection *Inside Outer Space*, Vas Dias finds them expressing "contempt, fury, ridicule, horror, amazement, tenderness, love, horniness, amusement, admiration" (xxxiii). And his list is far from complete. A tragedy like the *Challenger* explosion evokes not only sorrow but complex feelings of shame, disillusionment, and rage—feelings registered and explored by the poets.

Many poets do find the achievements of NASA worthy of celebration. Like Lindbergh's flight, the moon landing has been hailed as a triumph of the human spirit, with space exploration envisaged as an extension of earlier frontiers—a continuation, as Ronald Weber says, of our "national thrust into a regenerative unknown" (xii). But the paean to victory is not the dominant chord struck by American poets. Far more salient is their ambivalence toward the space program—so different from the poetic welcome given the invention of the airplane.

This reaction can be explained in many ways. In the 1960s, social ills claimed the headlines (poverty and racism at home, the Vietnam War abroad), making the $24-billion price tag of the Apollo missions look wildly extravagant. Planting an American flag on the lunar surface seemed to many observers an act of chauvinistic hubris. James Dickey, at first an enthusiastic proponent of the space program, came to believe that "this enormous and impressive 'step for mankind' is a triumph of the trivial" (*Sorties* 73).

But ambivalence to the space program went beyond sociology and politics. As May Swenson asks plaintively in her poem "Landing on the Moon," "Dare we land upon a dream?" (17). Poets mourned the loss of an ancient and cherished symbol. The mysterious moon goddess of so many myths—lovely, chaste, inspiring, eternally elusive—was, in July of 1969, reduced to a stony gray object of conquest. And conquest, not by a lone chivalric hero, but by a team, a whole NASA army of support personnel. Space victories are necessarily victories of technology, in which machines play the central role and humans follow procedures mapped out far in advance. As Weber observes, space flight is "one of the most regimented of human activities. Catastrophe is the only surprise" (xiii).

Perhaps in reaction to these uninspiring realities, many American poets turn away from the arid stones of the moon and the empty vastness of space. From a lunar perspective, they gaze anew at planet Earth, ponder its fragile beauty, its solitude, and embrace again its human delights and sorrows.

In recent years American writers like Philip Levine, Dick Allen, and Diane Ackerman have turned back in time as well, writing poems tinged with nostalgia for the early days of aviation and with appreciation for its more playful aspects, including the adventure of learning to fly. But in doing so, they have not returned to an outdated vocabulary of romanticism. At the close of the century, one hears in American poems of flight the emergence of a distinctly modern lyricism. The tone may be ironic or self-mocking, the rhythms and forms idiosyncratic, but a wealth of fresh images and innovative allusions attests a renewed allegiance to the fullness of language and its power to evoke and transform experience.

And what of the future? Is the airplane, like the locomotive, doomed to obsolescence or, at best, inconsequence? Robert Hedin, in *The Great Machines*, tells us that the poems of his anthology "chart the railroad's course from industrial innovation to a cultural phenomenon to its present status as a symbol of a vanishing way of life" (xv). Will nostalgia prove the prevailing mode of aeronautical verse? Might poets simply lose interest in aviation and space as significant themes for their work?

I think not. At the beginning of the twenty-first century the trajectory of both aviation and space exploration is clouded in uncertainty. And yet, as evident in the poems collected here, the dream of flight is deeply rooted in our human psyche, an archetypal image that manifests our deepest fears but also our transcendent hopes and aspirations. The airplane, as Goldstein points out, was "the indispensable symbol of American life in the twentieth century" (*Airplane* 248). The years ahead will surely show us new dimensions of air and space. And just as surely, a new generation of poets will emerge to trace for us the contrails of future flight.

In reading and reflecting on the poetry of flight, one discovers themes and images that echo from poem to poem, enriching them like a returning melody. The joys and terrors of the cockpit; the new perspectives opening outward and inward for the aerial passenger; the place of aviation in our earthbound lives, as we watch and wait for planes; the sinister role of the airplane in war; the shadow of airborne tragedy; the mythic dimensions of space flight—these overlapping themes define the six sections of *On the Wing*.

In selecting poems for inclusion, I have followed my own "passionate preferences," as Frost calls them, rejoicing in a striking image, in a richly connotative phrase, in a line that rings true. Literary merit has been the first criterion for selection, with only occasional exceptions made for a more ephemeral poem whose author or context gives it special interest. The date given for each poem represents that of its first publication (when known). Most of the works chosen speak clearly to the general reader, but for a few poems, brief notes at the end of the volume supply pertinent details. And for the reader wishing to pursue the connections between technological change and poetic response, "America in Flight" offers a summary of significant developments in the exploration of air and space.

PART ONE

Impulse of Delight

O to speed where there is space enough and air enough at last!
WALT WHITMAN from "Children of Adam" (1863)

We are the children of Science that mated
with Vision . . .
the riders of vapor . . .
the sowers of death . . .
the merchants of morrow . . .
the sellers of speed
FRANK ERNEST HILL from "The Flyers" (1925)

Ode for Orville and Wilbur Wright

I don't yearn for their steep excursion
Into fame and fortune, for it had
The usual price, and Orville died bitter
And Wilbur died young. I envy them
Only the slender and empty distance they left
Between them and a seaside's grassy bluffs
In mild December, the frail ingenuity
Of dreams, a lifetime's hopes made of string and cloth
And a little puttering motor that might have run
A lawnmower if the brothers had put their minds
To one first. For dumb exhilaration, nothing—
Not an F-16 thundering from its base
In Turkey, nor my red-eye circling O'Hare—
Comes close to what they must have felt
For less than a shaking, clattering minute,
Clearing all attachment to the world
Of dickering and petty concerns: for some,
No other heaven. So I take note of them
As they took notes from the lonely buzzard, obsessed
To the point of love with the ghostly air
And the small fluttering things that wandered
Through it. Eccentric but never flighty,
Bookish but not above nicking their hands
In bicycle shops and basements, they lived
With their sister and tinkered with the future.
Propelled by ambition, the mandate
It invents, they still heeded the laws
Of nature, trimmed needless weight, saw everything,
Even themselves, as burden, determined
Not to crash and burn. Sheer will launched them,
Good will, because those first forty yards

Skimming shale and reeds were for everyone.
Facedown between the struts, staring at the ground
As it blurred past, they failed like anyone
To grasp the implications. But legs flailing,
They hung on, buoyed by never and almost
And then just barely. I could do worse
Than their brief rapture, their common sense
Of purpose. Or I could, if only
For a moment, exalt them, go along
With the jury-rigged myth, the quaint
Contrivance that lets them rise above it all.

from Cape Hatteras

Stars scribble on our eyes the frosty sagas,
The gleaming cantos of unvanquished space . . .
O sinewy silver biplane, nudging the wind's withers!
There, from Kill Devil Hill at Kitty Hawk
Two brothers in their twinship left the dune;
Warping the gale, the Wright windwrestlers veered
Capeward, then blading the wind's flank, banked and spun
What ciphers risen from prophetic script,
What marathons new-set between the stars!
The soul, by naphtha fledged into new reaches
Already knows the closer clasp of Mars,—
New latitudes, unknotting, soon give place
To what fierce schedules, rife of doom apace!

Altitude

O the ten-, twelve-, twenty-story clouds
stacked due north of here,
my mother's mother's father in too-bright
ocean sunlight trying to teach angle and foil,
lift and flow, the sailshape of a wing.
Hard to imagine anything higher yet connected
or how the string tightens yet goes slack
at the rise and set,
the wind moving on a line like a wave.
Still alive, still coming down the stairs
learning to walk, bicycle clips and cap,
ready to ride the bike bought from the Wrights
in Dayton, eighteen-ninety something,
back in the ocean mist that rises behind us,
back to the boy, the Civil War, and school,
that face in the photo of the hundred-year-old soul.
Now bicycle wheels with wings, bicycle double gears
rising into the camera,
into the moment's white space,
the sea air's sudden history,
the shutter speed lifting just enough.
To stand on the coast of this part of Carolina
is to join the wind. In December,
the leeward to landward, shipwreck side.
For a man to fly he moves across and out and never stops.
Only Orville-in-the-air holds on, nineteen forty-eight,
the post-war Cold War year one of us survives.
The granite Wright Memorial the gravestone

where they start, first with the gliders,
then with the power, and tracks along a line to sail a train.
Someone taking pictures of the two flying kites—
boxy, triangular, sailcloth blown to rags—
that look like, in the blur of the turn of the century, ours.

The Poem of Flight

I shall begin with a rose for courage
and a rich green lawn where the crash occurs
with a sound like an old bridge gasping
under a load, and a white country house
from which a lady and her servants stream
toward the twisted moth. I would be
the original pilot, thirty-one, bare-headed,
my curly brown hair cut short and tinged
with blood from a wounded left hand
that must be attended to. Only an hour
before it was a usual summer morning,
warm and calm, in North Carolina,
and the two hectic brothers had laid aside
their bicycles and were busily assembling
the struts, wires, strings, and cranking
over the tiny engine. I faced the wind,
a cigarette in one hand, a map of creation
in the other. Silently I watch my hand
disappear into the white gauze the lady
turns and turns. I am the first to fly,
and the time has come to say something
to a world that largely crawls, forwards
or backwards, begging for some crust
of bread or earth, enough for a bad life
or a good death. I've returned because
thin as I am there came a moment
when not to seemed foolish and difficult
and because I've not yet tired
of the warm velvet dusks of this country
of firs and mountain oak. And because
high above the valleys and streams

of my land I saw so little of what is here,
only the barest whiff of all I eat each day.
I suppose I must square my shoulders,
lean back, and say something else,
something false, something that even I
won't understand about why some of us
must soar or how we've advanced beyond
the birds or that not having wings
is an illusion that a man with my money
refuses to see. It is hard to face
the truth, this truth or any other,
that climbing exhausts me, and the more
I climb, the higher I get, the less I
want to go on, and the noise is terrible,
I thought the thing would come apart,
and finally there was nothing there.

To Beachey, 1912

Riding against the east,
A veering, steady shadow
Purrs the motor-call
Of the man-bird
Ready with the death-laughter
In his throat
And in his heart always
The love of the big blue beyond.

Only a man,
A far fleck of shadow on the east
Sitting at ease
With his hands on a wheel
And around him the large gray wings.
Hold him, great soft wings,
Keep and deal kindly, O wings,
With the cool, calm shadow at the wheel.

The Coming of the First Aeroplanes

The coming of the first aeroplanes
out across America
obsesses me,
as other men are obsessed
by the President's face,
bi-sexual wives,
and I think *throttle stick, loop,*
barnstorm, goggles, dive,
shade my eyes
and all the doors
of all the houses open, and upon the small
lawns of 1920, people stand
praising God.
Satellites, the Venus probe, rim world,
teleport, dwarf stars, the luxon wall,
quasars, planetfall. I am
the first pilot from Boston.
Seeing a boy in a field,
I wave from the cockpit,
dip low my wings.
Aeroplanes.
They called them
crosses in the sky.

The Flight

An earthen shadow lay on men's endeavor.
Four years of war, nine years of bitter peace
Had bred a cynic wisdom in the young.
The old men fed
Upon the old thought: "Even the best are dead
"Soon and forever.
"Daily our power shrinks. Evils increase."
Some laughed, some cursed, some cried, but most were quiet,
Having drunk weak poisons till no potion stung.

Meanwhile the plunging hillocks of the sea
Skipped no less wildly because men were dull.
The mountains did not crane their craggy necks
To watch the cities climbing to their full
Desperate stature.
The wind was not still,
Ploughing the boughs for a harvest of rich sound,
Though no ear gathered it.

The stars were bound
On journeys that ignore the human will.
And clouds contended, and the soft rain fell,
And each neglected day that ended
Shed petals from the flowering immense
With a remote lavish indifference.

But that vast ocean, neither salt nor green,
That coastless sea where no ship voyages,
The nameless waters that the spirit knows,
Trembled like flesh under the lover's touch,
Trembled, unseen,

And shrank, and mightily rose . . .
Those cliffs, eternal and invisible,
That the soul pants for in the dread of death
As the sick stare at the health-giving hills,
Lifted their throats to the vehement proud breath
Of an announcing wind . . .
And music, thin as crystal snows,
Rang in that country where no man has been,
But where the pilgrim mind finds its profound repose.

Above the loud gray leagues of threatening sea,
Below the unfathomed ruthlessness of heaven,
But blind to both, having once turned the key
On light, on sound,
On every comradely
Solicitation of the day and night,
One flew, alone.
Locked in the narrow dark,
Seeing only the hands that passed across
This dial and that, to mark
Miles won, and power's loss,
As a physician feeling his own pulse
Might judge how soon no medicine would serve,–
He kept control
Of his dear monster: the enormous plane,
And of that singular passenger: his soul.
He was alone with it.
The cockpit held
Nothing but night, the roar of the machine,
The dials that said:
"So much is gone . . .
"There's storm ahead . . .
"So much is gone . . .
"There's storm behind . . .
"So much is gone . . ."

He was alone
As one condemned to die, whom neither friend
Nor stranger can commend
To the ambiguous Grace that chose to sow
Divine desires in man,—then lay him low.
In solitude, in darkness, and aware
Of a brute fury mastering the air
To its inane malignant ends,
He, in the air,
Pursued his course, prey to what agony
He need not say, nor on what victory's
Tremendous trail.
He flew, as toward a light
None the less luminous because it burned
Beyond the airy road his hooded eyes discerned.
He did not fail . . .

Not his far flight,
Not the dared feat and the accomplished goal,
Not the acclaiming thunders, nor the bright
And rapid rain of honors split the night
In which our coward courage, like a mole,
Crept stupidly, until he gave it eyes.
The miracle was wrought aloft, alone.
There in the upper reaches of the air,
With none to hear but his half-deafened soul,
Sounded the viking cry:
"Skoal, Lindbergh, skoal!"
The storm snarled vainly, and in vain the sea
Coiled back upon itself remorselessly.
Because one man was brave
At midnight, in mid-ocean, in mid-air,
The grave
Resigned its victory,
And death was robbed of its undying sting.

Here is the thing
That in the stress of mortal life stands firm,
Setting the lion's valor in the worm,
Pouring upon this jungle world a splendor
Larger than sunset fires, and more tender,
Showing to the mean heart and cruel mind
Provinces undiscovered, rich beyond imagination,
Not to be defined.

Humbly, as he,
And with the same smiling austerity,
Let us too fly
Through the known danger and the perils chanced,
Guessing what salty roadsteads, what grim sky
Regard our struggle. So we shall have danced
Our dance with fate, the Masqued One,
And have trodden
The windy spaces that the eagles tread.
"Even the best are dead
Soon" . . . But forever
Remembered virtue shines, and does not die.

wow

Courage

Courage is the price that life exacts for granting peace.
The soul that knows it not, knows no release
From little things;

Knows not the livid loneliness of fear
Nor mountain heights, where bitter joy can hear
The sound of wings.

How can life grant us boon of living, compensate
For dull gray ugliness and pregnant hate
Unless we dare

The soul's dominion? Each time we make a choice, we pay
With courage to behold resistless day
And count it fair.

Flight

for Amelia Earhart

A series of white squares, each
an hour's flying time, each with instructions
in pencil: the organized adventure. "Carelessness
offends the spirit of Ulysses." She suspends herself,
as he did, in the elements, finds
reason turns to motion, caution to design.
"One ocean led naturally to
another." Earth led naturally to sky
after a look at a thing of wood and wire
at the state fair in Des Moines, after the sting
of snow blown from the skis of training planes
near Philadelphia.
                  The rumble of the red and gold
Electra wakes the air, shakes stars
down their strings until
they hang outside the cockpit, close enough
to touch. Squares, like quickened days, take turns
showing her senses

what to do. The fragrance of blooming
orange orchards carries to considerable
altitudes. "No one has seen a tree
who has not seen it from the air, with
its shadow." Lake Chad is huge, shallow,
brightened by the wings of cranes and maribou
storks. The Red Sea is blue; the White and Blue Niles,
green; the Amazon delta a party of currents,
brown and yellow, distinct. Beyond

the clutter of sensations, the shriek and clatter
of tools at landing fields, she renews
herself, like the engine, for
one thing. Flight
above the wine-dark shining flood
is order, makes the squares
come and go, makes the plane
a tiny gear that turns the world. "Of all those things
external to the task at hand, we clutch
what we can."
                        She leaves the plane briefly to join
a crowd of Javanese walking up a volcanic mountain.
They laugh and talk, they carry baskets
and various loads on poles. "Sometime
I hope to stay somewhere as long as I like." For

the last long passage she abandons personal items,
souvenirs; also the parachute, useless over the Pacific.
The plane staggers with the weight of fuel,
becomes lighter and then
light. The last square has
an island in it, but cannot
lead her there.

Ascent

Plunge deep
Into the sky
O wing
Of the soul.

Reach
Past the last pinnacle
Of speech
Into the vast
Inarticulate face
Of silence.

Outleap
The turbulent gust
From forest,
Or the dust
Spiralling from the plain,
A yellow stain,
Swiftly erased again
In traceless tracts
Of space.

Up, up beyond
The giddy peaks of fear,
The glacial fields of doubt,
The sheer
Cliffs of despair;

Climb the steep stair
Of air.
There,

Where the gimlet screw
Of height-driven hawk
Pierces the blue,
Pursue!

There,
Where the wing
Has ceased to beat
For its own
Victory or defeat,

Find,
Far behind
The pale cloud-pastures
Of the mind,
The unbroken blind
Brightness of sheer
Atmosphere.

Here, crystalline,
Deep, full, serene,
Here flows
The still, unfathomed river
Of repose.

Here out of sight,
Unseen but known,
Here glides the stream
Of compassion.
Here alone
May rest
The strangled breast
Of long-impassioned flight.

Here soar
With more than wing
Above earth's floor;
Here ride
Limitless on a tide
No hawk has ever tried.

Here turn
In marble-firm
Security;
Here learn
To pivot on a needle-point—
Eternity.

Here whole
At last, above
The halting flight
That blindly rose
To gain a hidden height,

Wing of the soul
Repose,
Serene
In the stream
Of Love.

from The World Goes Black

DIVE FROM 45,000 FEET

Swathed in silence I drop,
the bones of my skull
thrumming against my brain.

Time is like an elastic band
the way it stretches and zings
back. My audience with the Holy Father—

four minutes, his chamberlain warned—
stretched into twenty-eight, passing
in one quick exhilarated gasp

while these forty-five seconds
slowed to cold molasses, time
enough to review a parade

of my life, catch destiny
waiting outside my cockpit
for one mistake, red-eyed

as the eject button. I fasten on
the machmeter, the needle
approaching and approaching,

like a body forging toward pleasure,
that point when I begin to beg
when nothing else matters

and the world goes black
as the world of the blind where touch
is everything, the only thing,
the thing next to holy.

Take-Off

He let go,
moving a racket
down the length of his mile-and-a-half concrete
farewell to Mother Earth, the faceless slabs
blinking, blurring, disappearing, till the black scabs
of oil and rubber blended and vanished
and he lifted sweet and clean and struck out
for always-autumned altitude,
the door of daystars,
the bird now less refractory
shinnying along on a long string of sky,
the priceless, skyscraping engine
turning brightly through its fearful chemistry,
thrusting the farm-quilts down, out and away
till all around for miles and miles and miles
that faded map of Texas lay majestic
far and away under the exotic metal
hissing and hung from the ox-straps of heaven.

Climbing Out

for Martin

Blue fluid in my limbs,
momentum buoys me up
at take-off speed
as I lose ground for that puzzle
older than hearsay,
whose thraldom is a witless bird
navigating a meadow.

Then, heavily afloat,
I run the river rapids
we know only by effect:
smoke chugging downwind,
apple boughs swinging
their fruit like censers,
the heat mirage gusty
over Lake Cayuga
when, as now, it's flat steel
burning in the sun.

Below me, planes sit nose up
on the airfield, like energy resting.
Only cloud-puffs
high above. At 3,000 feet,
hard atilt, I stall,
and a warning buzzer screams
like a marmoset loose
in the cabin, the hull trembles,
shudders twice, like a woman
gently coming, then nestles

straight down toward quilted green
and bedrock, till I get wind
of the right attitude
for lying long on the air,
and land like someone tripping
over toys in the darkness:
stagger, lurch, recovered fall.

But late at night,
still awake in the birdless,
starless black of my bedroom,
I am the moon
rinsed with glitter,
floating full over a pokey
and obedient land,
I am motion unmasked
by a wafer of steel,
I am lift made visible,
I am a dancer
with starched coat-tails for wings,
I am the mouth of a river
whose source is the sky,
I am trembling and hot
from this power-on stall,
I am flight-luscious,
I am kneeling on air.

DANIEL HOFFMAN (1968)

First Flight

I watches me climb
in the cockpit, him fixing
the belt and waving
my hand I see

the prop rev and the plane
cough forward
both wings biting
sudden wind

I on ground invisible
sees me taxi obvious
behind him Wild Pilot
what I doing there & here

particularly when
up high he says
Dan,
he says, Dan boy,

take over I don't feel
too good after all
that Scotch-type rot
last night I'm flying

me at the joystick o
boy how come
those chickens getting bigger chasing
their shadows under stoops

I see it clearly
clearly
STICK BACK!
and we climb

higher than the sun
sinking in a stew of clouds
Well Major anything
for a laugh me say

I says let's bring her down

Small Plane in Kansas

C'mon said the pilot and
the three of us climbed onto
the wing and into the snug plane.
With a short run we took off,
lurched upward, soared,
changed direction, missed a treetop,
and found an altitude.
Silo and wood below us
perfect toys, the field
so close you could see
the nested half-circles
where the tractor had turned in ploughing.

That's how it is in the flying dream,
where I step into a wind
with the seven-league boots of euphoria,
letting go, rising, each
pulse a step. Out there
from the height of self-love
I survey the reduced world.

Mastered by mastering,
I so much belong to the wind
I become of it, a gust
that flows, mindless for ever
along unmarked channel
and wall-less corridor where
the world's invisible currents run,
like symptoms, like remedies.

Tempus Fugit

for William Meredith

I

At half my age
sixty years ago
he flew among
the stars alone
in a black sky.

Perhaps he heard
the crack of radio
communication, perhaps
not, he kept himself
entertained, on course,
and finally, home.

II

I see him
eating a sandwich,
master of the seamless
ocean, plotting his way
by constellation:
like poetry,
a lonely business
like perhaps his dysphasia
or whatever hard human thing
you can imagine,

singing alone
with a sandwich
among the stars.

Those Who Wrestle with the Angel for Us

for Dion

I

My brother flies
A plane,
        windhover, night-lover,
Flies too low
Over the belled
        and furrowed fields,
The coiled creeks,
The slow streams of cars
        spilling
Like lust into the summer
Towns. And he flies
        when he
Should not, when
The hot, heavy air
        breaks
In storms, in high
Winds, when the clouds
        like trees
Unload their stony fruit
And batter his slender
        wings and tail.
But like the magician's
Dove, he appears home safely
        every time,
Carrying in his worn white
Bag all the dark
        elements

That flight knows,
The dark that makes

                his own soul

Dark with sight.

II

Even when he was a child, his skin was the white
Of something buffed by winds at high altitudes

Or lit by arctic lights—it gleamed like fish scales
Or oiled tin, and even then he wished to be alone,

Disappearing into the long grasses of the Ipperwash dunes
Where the gulls nested and where one afternoon

He fell asleep and was almost carried off by the sun—
In his dream he was running, leaping well, leaping

High as the hunted deer, and almost leaping free,
But like the tide, my gentle-handed mother hauled him back

With cold compresses and tea, and after that he favored
The dark, the ghostly hours, a small boy whistling in our yard

As he dragged a stick along the fence rails, and listened
To the slatted rattle of railroad cars, and knew by

Instinct how railroad lines look from the air, like ladders
Running northward to the stars, to the great constellations.

And he began then tracking his way through the names
Of all our fears, Cassiopeia, Andromeda, the shining Ram,

Tracking the miles and years he logs now, the lonely stretches
Where he finds the souvenirs that light our narrow kitchens—

Buckles and pins, watches and rings—the booty
That makes our land-locked, land-bound souls feel the compass

In our feet, and see in those who never speak, who
Slouch in with the dust of the northern wind on their backs,

The face of the angel we ourselves must wrestle with.

Flight Instructor

Sailplane, sliver of ice, seen
in the high window corner
peripheral to the road's way,
you dissolved on my tongue
between memory and desiring.
Your blade wing
cut a liminal cloud toward
the earlier boy, balsa
wings in hand, running
to learn the air. Roger,
when we were slanting
there, over the highway,
why was our sight no clearer?
My dream was ice, had asked
a white ascent
toward a higher father.

DAVID K. VAUGHAN (1973)

"A Lonely Impulse of Delight"—W. B. Yeats

for David Risher, who died in Vietnam

An airman must be Irish, slightly mad
To take that certain step that cancels all
The firm construction of an earthly stair,
And step to tread the thinner edge of air,
Where nothing yields support except the call
Of spirit in its element; who had
His start, perhaps, beneath an August night,
When, having seen the sign of Scorpio fixed
Among such suns, he seldom looked to earth
Again, unless to gain perspective when
He led his wingman toward the sun and then
Bent back to earth, then up again, to birth
A new maneuver of delight, to mix
The thought of man with sun, whose thought is light.

High Flight

Oh! I have slipped the surly bonds of Earth
    And danced the skies on laughter-silvered wings;
Sunward I've climbed, and joined the tumbling mirth
    Of sun-split clouds,—and done a hundred things
You have not dreamed of—wheeled and soared and swung
    High in the sunlit silence. Hov'ring there,
I've chased the shouting wind along, and flung
    My eager craft through footless halls of air. . . .

Up, up the long, delirious, burning blue
    I've topped the wind-swept heights with easy grace,
Where never lark, or even eagle flew—
    And, while with silent, lifting mind I've trod
The high untrespassed sanctity of space,
    Put out my hand and touched the face of God.

PART TWO

Worlds Above, Below, Within

High, pale, imperial places of slow cloud
And windless wells of sunlit silence . . .
FRANK ERNEST HILL from "Upper Air" (1928)

From this bird's-eye on high, I see . . . how the land recedes
     into shapes:
first the big agricultural patchwork, then commemorative stamps,
     then a weightless idea
above the clouds.
EMILY HEISTAND from "Regional Airport" (1995)

Imperial Airways

(London–Paris)

Black above the world
It flies
Like an anger
In the skies.

Seven years it cursed
The light;
Horror of a
Nameless night.

Now the triple engine
Roars;
And travelers (as a
Matter of course)

Eat their lunch and
Do not see
The earth's involved
Geometry.

To them the world below
Is some
Pattern of
Linoleum

To watch an hour or so
With eyes
Dead to distance
Or surprise,

Save (turning to their papers)
When
They read
The franc has fallen again.

THOMAS CARPER (1984)

An Aerial Photograph

He marvels at the regularity
Of fields, of fruit trees planted in long rows,
Of vines and hedges laid out mindfully.
The earthscape is an image of repose.
The roads are purposeful, going to town
Directly, bending only along the edge
Of too-high hills or, where the streams run down
The valley, organizing toward a bridge.
He thinks, "I have been there." When he was there,
He had been often lost. A patchwork land,
Odd curves in roads had kept him unaware
Of what, now, anyone could understand,
Looking at the aerial photograph
That shows no person on a human path.

Flight

Outside the porthole life, or what is
Not life streams in the air foils
Battering the wing tips, the houses
Small as in the skulls of birds, the frivolous ground

Of homes from which the force of motors
And the great riveted surfaces
Of the wings hold us, seated side by side
In flight, in the belly of force

Under the ceiling lights—the shabby bird
Of war, fear
And remoteness haunt it. We had made out
A highway, a city hall,

A park, but now the pastless ranches
Of the suburbs
Drift with the New World
Hills and the high regions

Which taken unaware
Resist, and the wings
Bend

In the open. Risk
And chance and event, pale
Ancestry beyond the portholes
Outside with the wings and the rivets.

Flying

We climbed the steps of air with motor roaring;
We entered silver portals, still unknown
To princes of the world, where stars were pouring
Their clustered flames like torches over-blown.
All night we wandered through the lofty halls
Of cloud—a palace builded in a dream
From mist and moonlight on whose shining walls
Strange phantoms of the sky like pictures gleam.
Then, as the zenith in a jeweled spire
Began to sparkle, down the icy dawn
We slipped to earth whose slowly kindled fire
In somber light among the trees was drawn:
But for us who had climbed the steps of air
Unreal was earth and insecure her stair.

Flying at Night

Above us, stars. Beneath us, constellations.
Five billion miles away, a galaxy dies
like a snowflake falling on water. Below us,
some farmer, feeling the chill of that distant death,
snaps on his yard light, drawing his sheds and barn
back into the little system of his care.
All night, the cities, like shimmering novas,
tug with bright streets at lonely lights like his.

from North

I. OVER PRAIRIE

Not in but past
the piled tumultuous torsos we
hummed, silvering in our plane
safe on course and

belted to set directions: not
for us the heave
of shoulders, shudder of pectorals
and massed forearms where

Buonarroti's chisel bit
the confining strap, and tissue and muscle swelled;
not for us the pitching
cumulus thighs, braced buttocks, hips

squared in Titan cloudshock
where giants strove: we
stayed steady, we
held fast to cups and tray tables, only tremors

shook us—which we ignored—
while sidewise the sky lunged,
towered and seared its own
brainpans in spasm

after spasm of struck light. It's possible
to watch. It's possible not
to be taken, not to be
touched. It's possible to fly

not in, but past—

Over Ohio

You can say what you want about the evils of technology
and the mimicry of birds: *I love it.* I love the sheer,
unexpurgated *hubris* of it, I love the beaten egg whites
of clouds hovering beneath me, this ephemeral Hamlet
of believing in man's grandeur. You can have all that
talk about the holiness of nature and the second Babylon.
You can stay shocked about the future all you want,
reminisce about the beauties of midwifery. I'll take this
anyday, this sweet imitation of Mars and Jupiter, this
sitting still at 600 mph like a jet-age fetus. I want to
go on looking at the moon for the rest of my life and seeing
footsteps. I want to keep flying, even for short distances,
like here between Columbus and Toledo on Air Wisconsin:
an Andean condor sailing over Ohio, above the factories,
above the dust and the highways and the miserable tires.

Flying Home from Utah

Forests are branches of a tree lying down,
its blurred trunk in the north.
Farms are fitted pieces of a floor,

tan and green tiles that get smoother,
smaller, the higher we fly.
Heel-shaped dents of water I know are deep

from here appear opaque, of bluish glass.
Curl after curl, rivers are coarse locks
unravelling southward over the land;

hills, rubbed felt, crumpled bumps
of antlers pricking from young bucks' heads.
Now towns are scratches here and there

on a wide, brown-bristled hide.
Long roads rayed out from the sores of cities
begin to fester and crawl with light—

above them the plane is a passing insect
that eyes down there remark, forget
in the moment it specks the overcast.

It climbs higher. Clouds become ground.
Pillows of snow meet, weld into ice.
Alone on a moonlit stainless rink

glides the ghost of a larva, the shadow
of our plane. Lights go on
in the worm-belly where we sit;

it becomes the world, and seems to cease
to travel—only vibrates, stretched out tense
in the tank of night.

The room of my mind replaces the long, lit room.
I dream I point my eye over a leaf
and fascinate my gaze upon its veins:

A sprawled leaf, many-fingered, its radial
ridges limber, green—but curled,
tattered, pocked, the brown palm

nibbled by insects, nestled in by worms:
One leaf of a tree that's one tree of a forest,
that's the branch of the vein of a leaf

of a tree. Perpetual worlds
within, upon, above the world, the world
a leaf within a wilderness of worlds.

Windowseat

Two hours out of Nairobi, distance
    unpeoples Ethiopian mountains to stark
        obsidian spines, black glass behind glass,

sliding blue sky. Then the Red Sea, not the pure
    aortal children picture
        drifting in its chamber torn

open, like a gift, but swirls
    ivory and lime green, low water rising
        over sand islands, round cells shivering

in a dish of sapphire jelly,
    that deep,

        deep water. Ending
in Jeddah's bone houses.
    Carved knuckles, tall fingers of mosques point

away from the city, straight up
    at us, our stiff wings, cups
        of coffee floating on trays. Compartments filled

with plastic masks, umbilical
    tubes of air.

    When we rise
too high, they tumble
    down to us, bring us back

    to ourselves, erase from our faces the pale
angelic blue.

A San Diego Poem: January–February 1973

THE JOURNEY BEGINS

My son tells his aunt,
"You take a feather,
and you have white stuff in your hand,
and you go outside,
and you let the white stuff fall to the ground.
That's praising."

In the morning, take cornfood outside,
say words within and without.
Being careful, breathe in and out,
praying for sustenance, for strength,
and to continue safely and humbly,
you pray.

SHUDDERING

The plane lifts off the ground.
The shudder of breaking from earth
gives me a split second of emptiness.
From the air, I can only give substance
and form to places I am familiar with.
I only see shadows and darkness
of mountains and the colored earth.

The jet engines drone heavily.
Stewardesses move along the aisles.
Passengers' faces are normally bland,
and oftentimes I have yearned, achingly,

for a sharp, distinctive face, someone
who has a stark history, even a killer
or a tortured saint, but most times
there is only the blandness.

I seek association with the earth.
I feel trapped, fearful of enclosures.
I wait for the Fasten Seat Belt sign
to go off, but when it does
I don't unfasten my belt.

The earth is red in eastern Arizona,
mesa cliffs; the Chinle formation
is an ancient undersea ridge lasting
for millions of years.
I find the shape of whale still lingers.
I see it flick gracefully by Sonsela Butte
heading for the Grand Canyon.

I recite the cardinal points of my Acoma life,
the mountains, the radiance coming
from those sacred points, gathering
into the center.
I wonder: what is the movement
of this journey in this jet above the earth?

Coming into L.A. International Airport,
I look below at the countless houses,
row after row, veiled by tinted smog.
I feel the beginnings of apprehension.
Where am I? I recall the institutional prayers
of my Catholic youth but don't dare recite them.
The prayers of my native selfhood
have been strangled in my throat.

The Fasten Seat Belt sign has come back on
and the jet drone is more apparent in my ears.
I picture the moments in my life
when I have been close enough to danger
to feel the vacuum prior to death
when everything stalls.
The shudder of returning to earth
is much like breaking away from it.

UNDER L.A. INTERNATIONAL AIRPORT

Numbed by the anesthesia of jet flight,
I stumble into the innards of L.A. International.
Knowing that they could not comprehend,
I dare not ask questions of anyone.
I sneak furtive glances at TV schedule consoles
and feel their complete ignorance of my presence.
I allow an escalator to carry me downward;
it deposits me before a choice of tunnels.
Even with a clear head, I've never been good
at finding my way out of American labyrinths.
They all look alike to me. I search
for a distinct place, a familiar plateau,
but in the tunnel, on the narrow alley's wall,
I can only find bleak small-lettered signs.
At the end of that tunnel, I turn a corner
into another and get the unwanted feeling
that I am lost. My apprehension is unjustified
because I know where I am I think.
I am under L.A. International Airport,
on the West Coast, someplace called America.
I am somewhat educated, I can read and use a compass;
yet the knowledge of where I am is useless.
Instead, it is a sad, disheartening burden.
I am a poor, tired wretch in this maze.

With its tunnels, its jet drones, its bland faces,
TV consoles, and its emotionless answers,
America has obliterated my sense of comprehension.
Without this comprehension, I am emptied
of any substance. America has finally caught me.
I melt into the walls of that tunnel
and become the silent burial. There are no echoes.

SURVIVAL THIS WAY

Survival, I know how this way.
This way, I know.
It rains.
Mountains and canyons and plants
grow.
We traveled this way,
gauged our distance by stories
and loved our children.
We taught them
to love their births.
We told ourselves over and over
again,
"We shall survive this way."

Our Ground Time Here Will Be Brief

Blue landing lights make
nail holes in the dark.
A fine snow falls. We sit
on the tarmac taking on
the mail, quick freight,
trays of laboratory mice,
coffee and Danish for
the passengers.

Wherever we're going
is Monday morning.
Wherever we're coming from
is Mother's lap.
On the cloud-pack above, strewn
as loosely as parsnip
or celery seeds, lie
the souls of the unborn:

my children's children's
children and their father.
We gather speed for the last run
and lift off into the weather.

On Hearing the Airlines Will Use a Psychological Profile to Catch Potential Skyjackers

They will catch me
as sure as the check-out girls
in every Woolworths have caught me, the badge
of my imagined theft shining in their eyes.

I will be approaching the ticket counter
and knowing myself, myselves,
will effect the nonchalance of a baron.
That is what they'll be looking for.

I'll say "Certainly is nice that the
airlines are taking these precautions,"
and the man behind the counter
will press a secret button,

there'll be a hand on my shoulder
(this will have happened before in a dream),
and in a back room they'll ask me
"Why were you going to do it?"

I'll say "You wouldn't believe
I just wanted to get to Cleveland?"
"No," they'll say.
So I'll tell them everything,

the plot to get the Pulitzer Prize
in exchange for the airplane,
the bomb in my pencil,
heroin in the heel of my boot.

Inevitably, it'll be downtown for booking,
newsmen pumping me for deprivation
during childhood,
the essential cause.

"There is no one cause for any human act,"
I'll tell them, thinking *finally*,
a chance to let the public in
on the themes of great literature.

And on and on, celebrating myself, offering
no resistance, assuming what they assume,
knowing, in a sense, there is no such thing
as the wrong man.

ANNA LEAHY (1996)

A History of Air Travel

In the beginning, all flight attendants were nurses,
nightingales, healers in motion above the earth.

Fear is the body's perception of altitude, flight's necessity.
Later, all they had to be was thin,

with height and weight the pretty margins of safety,
with a name that made them women.

Call button: a stick figure in a neat skirt, stewardess,
air hostess, a signal that we can get what we want easily.

Flight occurs only when both lift and thrust have won.
I want the impossible: to lift off from the ground

with uniformed guides, safe in our metal hull with its wings
     that cut
the clouds, splitting the air that closes back up,

smooth and thick with the earth's moisture,
as if it had not been cut at all, as if we had never sliced through.

Reading *Moby-Dick* at 30,000 Feet

At this height, Kansas
is just a concept,
a checkerboard design of wheat and corn

no larger than the foldout section
of my neighbor's travel magazine.
At this stage of the journey

I would estimate the distance
between myself and my own feelings
is roughly the same as the mileage

from Seattle to New York,
so I can lean back into the upholstered interval
between Muzak and lunch,

a little bored, a little old and strange.
I remember, as a dreamy
backyard kind of kid,

tilting up my head to watch
those planes engrave the sky
in lines so steady and so straight

they implied the enormous concentration
of good men,
but now my eyes flicker

from the in-flight movie
to the stewardess's pantyline,
then back into my book,

where men throw harpoons at something
much bigger and probably
better than themselves,

wanting to kill it, wanting
to see great clouds of blood erupt
to prove that they exist.

Imagine being born and growing up,
rushing through the world for sixty years
at unimaginable speeds.

Imagine a century like a room so large,
a corridor so long
you could travel for a lifetime

and never find the door,
until you had forgotten
that such a thing as doors exist.

Better to be on board the *Pequod,*
with a mad one-legged captain
living for revenge.

Better to feel the salt wind
spitting in your face,
to hold your sharpened weapon high,

to see the glisten
of the beast beneath the waves.
What a relief it would be

to hear someone in the crew
cry out like a gull,
Oh Captain, Captain!
Where are we going now?

Flying, Reflying, Farming

We are flying white air. The most pioneering
falcon of all is hopelessly beneath us.
Nothing above but sky bleached out
by the sun's remorseless hammering
through ozone. Our lives inch back below,
the farm gray because a cruel past, weather
or mother, turns the spirit gray. The oldest
daughter left one day for good. The first son
(how can I know this at this altitude)
is trapped for life. At best, he can only get rich.
What good reason could the pilot have
for suddenly pointing the plane at the sun
and cutting the power? I hear his
hysterical laughter all the air down
to rock. We implode into acres
of black we rehearsed every young rage.
Another farm, tiny as the attendant's voice
on the defective intercom slips back
beneath us, bright orange this time and home.
We are flying white air.

The aluminum creaks. The wing shudders.
We are flying rough air. Remember
the wing snapping back over Europe
(where was that?), the agonizing sheer
you saw in slow motion, the vomit
you held back with prayer, and your friend
spinning down fatal ether
man had no business in. Back at the base
you were sobbing fields away from the rest
and the shepherd in black offered you pears

and wouldn't take your money. You claimed
you paid him with tears but that made no sense.
The air is solid again. We eat our way north.
We are flying good air.

We have entered the pattern.
Power reduced. Flaps down. Seat belt sign on.
In a moment, no smoking. This is always
a major kind of return. Thirty years ago
we came down and laughed and shook hands
after a rough one. We congratulated ourselves
for being alive. Long before that
we were ignorant farmers. Remember the night
you came home cheated in town of the money
you'd saved to paint the farm green.
Your wife called you weak and you stammered
and wept. Late one morning years later,
drunk and alone, you remembered above us
air is white, and you knew your next wife
would forgive you, your crops come
fatter than clouds, old friends return.
We have landed on schedule. Reverse thrust.
We are safe. We are natural on earth.

United Flight 608

Up ahead, First Class
Gets free scotch and stewardesses
A little tenderer.
Otherwise, it's the same.

The old lady beside me
May be visiting grandchildren
For whom she brings
No wisdom.

Businessmen as pensive
As elegiac poets, stare out
The windows. Someone says those calm
Unearthly lights below
Are Omaha.

The pilot also waits
For his instructions,
And the poor
Ride under the dark
In buses.

What's happened before
And will again because
Necessary: gliding on into port
At night, oars lifted
Over black water,
Abashed,
But too tired at last to explain.

Ten thousand years traveling
And I've learned nothing.

Airplane

Up here, where no Indian was ever meant to be
I carry the small and usual things for safety:

generic novel, movie magazine, book of poems
by the latest great poet, bottle of water, and faith

or guilt, depending on the amount of turbulence.
Like everyone else, I believe in God most

when I'm closest to death. How did I become this
Catholic and catholic, wanting to get to Heaven

as painfully and quickly as everyone else?
Maybe I can look out the window and see God

sitting on the wing. Maybe God is in First Class
enjoying a complimentary carafe of red wine.

"If God is on the plane," I told the flight attendant,
"then I am safe." "However," she said, "I don't think

God is on the passenger list." "I just want
to know who has the best chance of saving my life,"

I asked the flight attendant. "The pilot," she said
but it sounded exactly like she said I could survive

any wreck if I said the last word of my latest prayer
at the exact moment of impact. How did I become this

Indian flying from one anonymous city to another?
They're all anonymous to me. I can't tell

the difference between New York City and Eugene, Oregon.
I woke up one morning in Tulsa and cried

for all the losses, the bleached bones of buffalo
buried out there on the Great Plains, then realized

I was still in San Francisco, waiting for the earthquake
and wanting it to reveal the bones of all the prisoners

drowned and concealed during that long swim
between Alcatraz and the shore. We are all prisoners.

How did I become this poor Indian with his hands folded
into fists, into a tightly wound prayer, as air became ground

and this airplane, my airplane, landed safely
in a light rain? I walked down the stairs, dis-

embarked, and asked the ground crew if they knew
why this Indian was in the exact place

where no Indian was ever meant to be.
"Engineers," they said, but it sounded exactly

like they said there is a thin, unwavering line
between God and the next available flight.

How did I become this crazy
Catholic who steals the navigational flags

and races down the runway, waving at them all, all
those planes trafficking in the dusky sky? I count

one, two, up to seven planes. I count and count.
I wave those flags (I want to light fires) and I wave

those flags (I want to light fires). I want
to bring all of those planes in, bring them all in

even though each plane might contain a madman
because each plane might instead contain the woman

who wants to light a fire. I stand on the runway waving
them all in, with my left arm like this and my right arm

frantic, wanting to know how I became like this,
just like this, wanting to bring everybody back home.

FLT #4372

You pray. You forgive your enemies.
You love your children with unnatural fierceness,
imagining them growing up parentless.

You make promises. You admire the ground,
you adore it—even those wrinkled hills
strewn with debris—it dawns on you—

debris like the wreckage of a plane!
And that's how you find yourself entering
the mind's eye of your own death. Kneeling

beside your body, down there, the sensible fingernails,
the fine wrinkles, the bones that never let you down—
you feel the terror of losing everything.

Then mystery opens its parachute in you,
whispering, *You're still here.* You can't imagine
what it means. But with one finger you shut

your body's eyes like shutting the covers of
a novel so satisfying you'll never read it again.
Around you, the others are kneeling

beside themselves. Each one is a little tent
pitched on the hillside. It is spring
and you have all just been born.

With all your practicing of death, you could never
have guessed this, how aroused you feel
and wild for whatever comes next. Meanwhile,

as if in a dream, the stewardess smiles at you
and nudges the steel cart down the aisle.
The plane plunges forward miraculously,

leaving your body on the hillside below,
overshooting your death, somehow,
the sky, blue as mercy, not explaining.

At the Controls

manning the controls, faith
is required, instruments
must perform, the slightest
nudge on the joystick
to keep on course
for the rush at touchdown

figures from the past
flicker in front of me,
hands waving hello
or goodbye? the re-run
I'm always playing
without clothes on
friends around me
lurching as we
hurtle down the open
tarmac, hangups forgotten

let us ride the airwaves
open up conversations
beyond the cockpit
seize the hands
that reach out to us,
forget the fallibility
of engines bearing us up
that could let us down
why not believe that forward
movement will keep us
buoyant: a will, a kind of act

Landing

On the way down through clouds,
the plane shudders. This is the moment,
isn't it, when we wonder about our lives.
What haven't we done? Who will miss us, really?

Then lights, a gentle touchdown,
the quiet grip of earth that fixes us to a place.
And we make a choice—to live
where we were, or where we are now.

A Hmong woman sits across the aisle,
round face, gold skin,
braids folded up in a black knit hat.
Her feet don't touch the floor,
yet her body seems to believe this destiny.
When she stands, she's straight,
though her cap rubs arms with a world so strange
her grandchildren will be as tall as mine.

I follow her across the threshold.
Many languages flare up around us,
somehow all of them familiar—
arrivals, departures, a welcome home.

She is greeted by her family, speaking Hmong.
And you, and I, feel under our feet
the rise of a new language.

We have landed now.

PART THREE

Airplane Visions, Airport Truths

Sail forth, winged Argonauts of trackless air . . .
Man's Brotherhood, bring *that* as Golden Fleece
On sun-blessed wings, bright harbingers of peace.
CHARLES L. EDHOLD from "Wings" (1909)

Brilliant, dashing, wingèd thing . . .
Moving there across the sky,
What new message do you bring?
ANONYMOUS (1910)

Remember those wingovers and loops and spins?
Forbidden. Heavy, powerful, and solemn,
Our scheduled transports keep the straight and level.
It's not the joystick now, but the control column.
HOWARD NEMEROV "The Dream of Flying Comes of Age" (1967)

Airports.
Such lonely places!
People shuffling through, baggage-bent,
With vacant destinations mirrored in their eyes.
CLAYTON SNEDEKER from "Terminals" (1973)

The Unconquered Air

I

Others endure Man's rule: he therefore deems
   I shall endure it—I, the unconquered Air!
   Imagines this triumphant strength may bear
His paltry sway! yea, ignorantly dreams,
Because proud Rhea now his vassal seems,
   And Neptune him obeys in billowy lair,
   That he a more sublime assault may dare,
Where blown by tempest wild the vulture screams!

Presumptuous, he mounts: I toss his bones
   Back from the height supernal he has braved:
Ay, as his vessel nears my perilous zones,
I blow the cockle-shell away like chaff
   And give him to the Sea he has enslaved.
He founders in its depths; and then I laugh!

II

Impregnable I held myself, secure
   Against intrusion. Who can measure Man?
   How should I guess his mortal will outran
Defeat so far that danger could allure

For its own sake?—that he would all endure,
   All sacrifice, all suffer, rather than
   Forego the daring dreams Olympian
That prophesy to him of victory sure?

Ah, tameless courage! dominating power
That, all attempting, in a deathless hour
   Made earth-born Titans godlike, in revolt!–

Fear is the fire that melts Icarian wings:
Who fears not Fate, nor Time, nor what Time brings,
   May drive Apollo's steeds, or wield the thunderbolt!

The Aeronauts

How will they look upon us wingless ones,
Our great aerial children soon to come,
Who even now begin to quicken life
With movement toward their finer element,
And fierce essays against the weight of Time?
When, in the weary lapse of some long flight,
Dawn, undisturbed of any lifting leaf,
Uninterrupted of a waking bird,
Shakes its vast silence in among the stars,
Will they not turn from radiant tides of light,
And, steering earthward, softly speak of us
Their fathers, long contented under trees?
Yet who shall blame them if they soon forget?
The sunlight will be woven in their blood,
And breadth of spaces, native to their breath,
Will urge them till they soar again for joy.
To them the hills will rise no more, but knit
By river-threads of silver to the vales,
Will trace one pattern to the fringing seas.
Down, ever downward, floats earth's tapestry!
Its mountain folds to emerald ripples smoothed
By intervening heights of azure air.
Up, up they mount! Where never eagle's wing
Drops feather; or the smallest waft of cloud
Casts its translucent shadow; till the line
Of earth's horizon brims a cup so huge
Its rim dissolves the endless distances
In purple interminglings of faint mist.
And there, within the Garden of the Skies,
With Heaven above, and heaven, as fair, below,
Only the winds, forever voicelessly

Astir among the daffodils of morn
Or soft in petals of the sunset rose,
Recall them to those meadows whence they sprung.
Cloud-cradled must the youth, indeed, have been,
And intimate with starry altitudes,
Whose song would venture that new Paradise,
Or lips attempt that greater Adam's fame
Who pioneered against the rising sun
And staked his claim above the rainbow's sign.
But unto us, the wingless, in our dreams
May come a faint prevision of that hour
On cloudless mornings after days of rain;
Or from some mountain summit's lift of snow;
Or in a sunset reddening far at sea
The moment may be miraged. And our hearts,
Now islanded by little miles of grass
And tiny leagues of waving forest leaves
Into dissenting nations, leap to meet
A future wherein unfenced realms of air
Have mingled all earth's peoples into one
And banished war forever from the world.
Yet seldom dare we dream of such a dream
Lest we despair that we must die too soon.

ROLAND FLINT (1965)

August from My Desk

It is hot today, dry enough for cutting grain,
And I am drifting back to North Dakota
Where butterflies are all gone brown with wheat dust.

And where some boy,
Red-faced, sweating, chafed,
Too young to be dying this way,
Steers a laborious, self-propelled combine,
Dreaming of cities, and blizzards—
And airplanes.

With the white silk scarf of his sleeve
He shines and shines his goggles,
He checks his meters, checks his flaps,
Screams contact at his dreamless father,
He pulls back the stick,
Engines roaring,

And hurtles into the sun.

An October Nocturne

October 31st, 1936

The night was faint and sheer;
Immobile, road and dune.
Then, for a moment, clear,
A plane moved past the moon.

O spirit cool and frail,
Hung in the lunar fire!
Spun wire and brittle veil!
And trembling slowly higher!

Pure in each proven line!
The balance and the aim,
Half empty, half divine!
I saw how true you came.

Dissevered from your cause,
Your function was your goal.
Oblivious of my laws,
You made your calm patrol.

The Buzz Plane

May my Irish grandfather from Tyrells Pass
Grant me the grace to make a proper curse on you, accursed!
You who on a holy Sabbath or a fair holiday
Buzz and circle above my head like the progeny
Of the miscegenation of a buzzard and a bumble-bee.

The great bombers I hate with a lofty hatred,
But you, Harpy, with your unspeakable clatter,
Your sputtering, stuttering, and you know what,
Queering both my music and my silence,
I despise as the perfection of pure nuisance.

Where is the wind-wailed island of mist and seagulls,
Where is the mountain crag mounting to eagles,
Where is the saint's cell, the hermit's citadel,
The nine bean rows and the hive for the honey bee,
Safe from your snoopings, swoopings, and defilements?

May your wife be a gad, a goad, and a gadfly.
May all your bawling, brawling brats never leave you peace.
May you grow bald and birds defile your head.
May your flights be tailspins and your landings crashes.
Fie, fie, fie on you! And the word has power!

Jet Plane

Stung by the tail of a scorpion
Gravity loosens its grip
On the side of a hellion
Who scorches the sky
Through a curve of silence
While sound tumbles backward
In the tangled air.

The monster with open mouth
Sucks food from runnels of light
Washing blue space
Through a furious gut.

Tiptoe on the flattened world
The watchers are asking their eyes
If a dragon that swallows flame
Can burrow a hole
In the sagging roof of the morning.

Upon a ladder of smoke
The monster touches the zenith
But gravity roused from its spell
Reaches toward rafters of sunlight
And drags the scorpion down
To a crevice of earth.

Air Show

(Hanscom Field, Bedford, Mass.)

In shapes that grow organic and bizarre
Our Air Force ramifies the forms of war.
The stubby bomber, dartlike fighter yield
To weirder beasts caught browsing on this field,
With wry truncated wings, anteater snouts,
And burnished bellies full of ins and outs.
    Caressing curves of wind, the metal smiles
And beds the pilot down in sheets of dials.
Eggheaded, strapped, and sucking gas, he roars
To frozen heights all other life abhors,
Where, having left his dirty sound behind,
In pure blue he becomes pure will and mind.
    These planes, articulate in every part,
Outdo the armor-forger's Tuscan art—
The rivets as unsparingly displayed
As pearls upon a chasuble's brocade,
The wiring bundled thick, like chordate brains,
The posing turbine balanced grain by grain,
The silver skin so stencilled it amounts
To an encyclical of do's and don't's.
    Our dollars! Dumb, like muzhiks come from far
To gaze upon the trappings of a czar,
Their sweat turned into gems and cold faïence,
We marvel at our own extravagance:
No mogul's wasteful lust was half so wide
And deep as this democracy's quick pride.

Air Show: F-16s above Cleveland

Clearly, we are a part of the performance, slowing our
cars on the freeway, errands interrupted
like dull dreams of waking, taking a shower,
interrupted by the true alarm. The solo jets
low above, turning into some trick, some loop or roll
we can't see through the towers of downtown—
just the roar chasing the flash of plane,
catching it overhead. Then the diamond of jets
needling through smokestacks, wing to wing, using principles
    of trust
I don't understand, but I understand this—
not *pilot* or *engine* or *maneuver*—
the trick here is panic, and I play along—Dear whomever:

spare this city, slow to recover, our hazy old sky.
Spare our lives awaiting attack. Spare our somnambulant cars.

Watching the Planes Come In at La Guardia

Joan's kiss
      —it pancakes—
            a flat smack.

                    But Jeanne!
The delicate approach, slow tilt and lean.
All hovering danger and delight.
              As when
Home, over mountain, sea, and chancy weather,
Plane and its shadow
        thrill
          and touch together.

Dragon-watching in St. Louis

for Stephen, Geoffrey, Vanessa, Lawrence

It would have been a dragon, this monstrous jet,
two hundred years ago, to father and little boy
come out for a stroll, had they seen it go screeching down
into the sunset with sweptback wings downglinting
as their words rose like drowned twigs from a stream,
the little boy exclaiming, the father agreeing.
They would have fled in terror what we take in stride
since we live near an airport and have rendezvoused
with sun and horizon here too often to fear
that this great beast might shatter, his smoky fires dim
the park, touched by the sun's last shining, we've come to see.

By the dark-mortared wall, whose chalk-white stones protect
this place from the fuming roaring freeway just beneath us,
we can look far over the asphalt and across suburban roofs
and see how the jetplane now small and tranquil is sinking,
winking the ruby of its landing light, in the last
seconds before it touches the earth beneath our horizon—
and we listen until it's come safely down like the sun,
till silence tells us it's landed, as darkness tells
that the trillion hydrogen bombs of our sun eyeballing space
to light and warm us this day have held their peace,
as firmness tells feet that the earth, whose sensitive crust's
light quiver would bury us in our buildings, now smoothly
turns on appointed rounds as it brings this smoky city
gliding through sunset into starlit night as that dazzle of
cars weaving through traffic snarls, homing on supper smells,
tells us it's time to be strolling back home on the safe

sidewalks of this suburb
                    where bears and panthers, flood
and fire and that fearful monster the Wild Osage, whose blood
runs in our veins, ranged these savage woodlands hundreds
of years ago, before the walks were made safe for us to enjoy
this zoo of smoky dragons now swarming from our best brains.

At a Motel near O'Hare Airport

I sit by the window all morning
watching the planes make final approaches.
Each of them gathers and steadies itself
like a horse clearing a jump.

I look up to see them pass,
so close I can see the rivets
on their bellies, and under their wings,
and at first I feel ashamed,
as if I had looked up a woman's skirt.

How beautiful that one is,
slim-bodied and delicate
as a fox, poised and intent
on stealing a chicken
from a farmyard.

And now a larger one, its
tail shaped like a whale's.
They call it sounding
when a whale dives,
and the tail comes out of the water
and flashes in the light
before going under.

Here comes a 747,
slower than the rest,
phenomenal, like some huge
basketball player
clearing space for himself
under the basket.

How wonderful to be that big
and to fly through the air,
and to make such a big shadow
in the parking lot of a motel.

The Sparrows at the Airport

Their brown, harmless flack
Which bursts in feathery chirrupings
About the apron, stings
The eye with what they lack

Of speed and power. Their size,
Suitable to glean the crumbs
Of great flight, humdrums
Brown earth into their lives.

Yet over the field they break
Gustily tumbled up to try
Ambitious missions by
Deliberate mistake.

So one must think them pressed
To know the promise if they fall,
The way their careless small
Flight puts it to test.

Meteoric blue
Spans of silver daze the air
About them. Runways flare
To giant craft that prove

Their slight inconsequence,
And all seems scheduled to decree
Their humility
Amid new monuments.

But there, as if to sing
Election from their minute conclave,
They chatter and perch, brave
What short chance may bring,

And watch the liners landing
Safe against imponderable odds,
With quick, indifferent nods
And rare understanding.

The Unwingèd Ones

I don't travel on planes.
I travel on trains.
Once in a while, on trains,
I see people who travel on planes.
Every once in a while I'm surrounded
By people whose planes have been grounded.
I'm enthralled by their air-minded snobbery,
Their exclusive hobnobbery,
And I'll swear to, before any notary,
The clichés of their coterie.
They feel that they have to explain
How they happen to be on a train,
For even in Drawing Room A
They seem to feel déclassé.
So they sit with portentous faces
Clutching their attaché cases.
As the Scotches they rapidly drain
That they couldn't have got on the plane,
They grumble and fume about how
They'd have been in Miami by now.
They frowningly glance at their watches,
And order more Scotches.
By the time that they're passing through Rahway
They should be in Havana or Norway,
And they strongly imply that perhaps,
Since they're late, the world will collapse.
Then, as station merges with station,
They complain of the noise and vibration.
These outcasts of aviation,
They complain of the noise and vibration.
Sometimes on the train I'm surrounded

By people whose planes have been grounded.
That's the only trouble with trains;
When it fogs, when it smogs, when it rains,
You get people from planes.

At the Airport

Through the gate, where nowhere and night begin,
A hundred suddenly appear and lose
Themselves in the hot and crowded waiting room.
A hundred others herd up toward the gate,
Patiently waiting that the way be opened
To nowhere and night, while a voice recites
The intermittent litany of numbers
And the holy names of distant destinations.

None going out can be certain of getting there.
None getting there can be certain of being loved
Enough. But they are sealed in the silver tube
And lifted up to be fed and cosseted,
While their upholstered cell of warmth and light
Shatters the darkness, neither here nor there.

Dulles Airport

Detached by Saarinen or God
from all coordinates,
it sits like a gull upon water
defying the subtle Archimedean rule.

The earth flows without displacement.
In this the only measured space of the world,
we come each a half two hundred yards
from shadow to form
from form to person, to meet
within the green range of each other's sight.

There at the center point, at midnight,
no arrivals or departures scheduled,
ticket sellers and stewardesses sleep,
planes and pilots are released.

Into this innocence of light,
not one eye of the myriad-eyed mankind
dares look. Let us dance, slowly turning.
We are seen by the immodest,
unlidded, unblinking, snake-eyed electric beam.
The door opens out. Not driven
but drawn by darkness, we go
naked into the immeasurable night.

Kennedy Airport

Those greetings! those goodbyes!
I am passing Kennedy Airport—would know it blindfold
by the glad snarl of jets.
Many times, living near, we told each other:
One night, let's take off and arrive
with those great dragons!
Let's watch some families
go through their griefs, their joys!
Now the terminals are blended in my head,
and our passengers—going, coming—and the years;
arrivals too late, departures too early,
meeting places botched,
fragile names blared like hospital personnel . . .
only the pattern is clear:
children wrenched away, and again, again,
wrenched away, after each crumb of a visit,
to Chicago, Ann Arbor, finally Kermanshah,
our noses rubbed in the fact, again and again,
that they were not part of the unit any more,
that the nest was down to two . . .
and other arrivals, other departures,
always with huggings, tears;
always a clutching, not a clasping of hands.

I cannot pass Kennedy Airport without aching,
though for us it means greetings as well as goodbyes
—unlike my grandmother, she who coughed forth her soul
in the back of a wagon alone
on her way to a doctor too late
on a snow-cursed Polish road
without a goodbye from her husband

(but greeted by God at least, I would like to believe);
unlike my grandmother, who never did make it to America
where I hoped all my young years to greet her,
and who never even came to the depot
on those five nightmare mornings
as her children were wrenched away,
goodbye after goodbye,
depot with no greetings, only goodbyes,
till her nest was down to two,
without ever one telephone syllable to breathe or receive,
one word to decipher or place on a postcard;
waiting, waiting for the steerage tickets
her five American children and their mates
never did grow quite prosperous enough to send.

Airport

None of the computers can say
how long it took to evolve a facility
devoted to absence in life

you walk out of the chute
and a person smiles at your ticket
and points you to your seat

is this the only way home
nobody asks
because nobody knows

the building is not inhabited it is not
home except to roaches
it is not loved it is serviced

it is not a place
but a container with signs
directing a process

there is neither youth in the air
nor earth under foot
there is a machine to announce

yet the corridors beat with anguish longing relief
news trash insurance dispensers
and many are glad to be here

thinking of being somewhere else
hurrying at great expense
across glass after glass

we travel far and fast
and as we pass through we forget
where we have been

Bad Weather at the Airport

I watch through walls of windows where the rain
shatters against the airport's outside lights.
Thunderstorms move between us, you in your plane
beyond their reach, adrift in starry night,
while I subtract a hundred minutes from
every hour. I read the lightning's signs
written in clefts of mammoth clouds that come
and go as thunder detonates its mines.
I wait for quaking winds to disappear,
the rush of surf on windows to grow still,
the darkness in my deepest self to clear.
Swept by the tides of emptiness that fill
the space between us, I strive toward the shore,
the wonder of your coming through the door.

Vacation

I love the hour before takeoff,
that stretch of no time, no home
but the gray vinyl seats linked like
unfolding paper dolls. Soon we shall
be summoned to the gate, soon enough
there'll be the clumsy procedure of row numbers
and perforated stubs—but for now
I can look at these ragtag nuclear families
with their cooing and bickering
or the heeled bachelorette trying
to ignore a baby's wail and the baby's
exhausted mother waiting to be called up early
while the athlete, one monstrous hand
asleep on his duffel bag, listens,
perched like a seal trained for the plunge.
Even the lone executive
who has wandered this far into summer
with his lasered itinerary, briefcase
knocking his knees—even he
has worked for the pleasure of bearing
no more than a scrap of himself
into this hall. He'll dine out, she'll sleep late,
they'll let the sun burn them happy all morning
—a little hope, a little whimsy
before the loudspeaker blurts
and we leap up to become
Flight 828, now boarding at Gate 17.

At the Terminal

Remember when we took those separate flights
imagining the worst: our children robbed
of parents, both at once? I'd leave an hour
before you, wait to meet you at your gate,
or you'd go first, arrive and rent a car,
then meet me at the exit. In between,
blue emptiness, our lives suspended where
clouds stacked themselves between us: you on earth
and I already gone. Or else I'd stand
on solid ground and watch you disappear—
my heart, my shining bird!—a streak of light,
a flash of wing, then nothing. Only one
of us, one at a time. And whether I turned
back to the concourse or pulled down the shade
over the brilliant window, belted in
above the tilting tarmac, I rehearsed
this hour, ever nearer, when the planet
would hold one or the other, and you'd watch—
or I—the earth receding, or look up
into the arc of absence, blinding space.

Passengers

At the gate, I sit in a row of blue seats
with the possible company of my death,
this sprawling miscellany of people—
carry-on bags and paperbacks—

that could be gathered in a flash
into a band of pilgrims on the last open road.
Not that I think
if our plane crumpled into a mountain

we would all ascend together,
holding hands like a ring of skydivers,
into a sudden gasp of brightness,
or that there would be some common place

for us to reunite to jubilize the moment,
some spaceless, pillarless Greece
where we could, at the count of three,
toss our ashes into the sunny air.

It's just that the way that man has his briefcase
so carefully arranged,
the way that girl is cooling her tea,
and the flow of the comb that woman

passes through her daughter's hair . . .
and when you consider the altitude,
the secret parts of the engines,
and all the hard water and the deep canyons below . . .

well, I just think it would be good if one of us
maybe stood up and said a few words,
or, so as not to involve the police,
at least quietly wrote something down.

Jet Lag

From the desert west we jet back east
Where it's already rainy, dark and cold.

We swap the palms for spanish moss.
Home, unpacking, I still see desert

Stars as secondary to the dark,
To parents alone and distant again.

It's bedtime here, time for dinner there:
I can still see mountains in their window—

Old, they survive just fine on their own,
Get plenty of attention from cameras.

When he's sick he doesn't speak and when
He doesn't speak, I'm all alone for days.

My family has settled into sleep upstairs.
By myself, I've never been less alone.

Now I know how the Word can save
And let that gospel word itself in her lap

As always. Altar boys advance in white,
Nuns, priests from an unbelievable parish . . .

I can't sleep—I'm still in a different time.

PART FOUR

Angle of Attack

Angle of Attack is the angle at which the wing meets the air . . .
the most important fact in the art of piloting.
WOLFGANG LANGEWIESCHE from "Stick and Rudder" (1944)

For the fighter pilot it means everything. Dogfights, spins, dives—
if you've got the right angle of attack, you won't stall, you won't
exceed the limits of your airplane, you won't kill yourself. And
it's not just a technique, it's a way you face life.
CAPTAIN DORI A. KANELLOS from "Angle of Attack" (2003)

And memory, that makes things miniature
And far away, and fit size for the mind,
Returned him in the form of images
The size of flies, his doings in those days

With theirs, the heroes that came out of the sun
To invent the avant-garde war of the air—
HOWARD NEMEROV from "Models" (1987)

Eagle Youth

They have taken his horse and plume,
They have left him to plod, and fume
For a hero's scope and room!
They have curbed his fighting pride,
They have bade him burrow and hide
With a million, side by side:
     Look—into the air he springs,
     Fighting with wings!

He has found a way to be free
Of that dun immensity
That would swallow up such as he:
Who would burrow when he could fly?
He will climb up into the sky
And the world shall watch him die!
     Only his peers may dare
     Follow him there!

About Eyes

The terror of the serene plane is in their eyes:
look deeply, see the wings dip, and the revolving nose

split sky and cloud, ten thousand feet above
the remembered city of women with violent hearts,

incredibly aged children, dark-eyed, who recall
the propeller's sound and the panic
from the days of the womb's darkness.

The eyes contain, reflect more than the image photographed
in the almanacs, the newspapers, the albums airmen are fond of.

The joy of the plunge through mist into sun is unknown to
the wide anonymous eyes of the dwellers in bombed cities.

The eyes reveal everything: the inhuman grace
of the silver flight, and the first melodic hum,
deceitful, cruel, of the synchronized guns and motors

and the arc-plummet fall of the bombs, the grotesque explosion,
the hysteria of the insane siren, the last deception.

A Leaf from a Log Book

Dropping down through tired skies;
The wires sighing above the propeller-whispers;
The cooling wind pouring over the windshield glass;
Our ships are dropping into the valley
Over the gleaming tile of scattered roof-tops
    And abbey spires.

A moon, already far beyond the last retreat of day,
    Is rising in its bloom.
We are sleek carnivorous birds
Whistling down to a haven among the hills,
Our bodies gorged with the blood of legions.

The Fury of Aerial Bombardment

You would think the fury of aerial bombardment
Would rouse God to relent; the infinite spaces
Are still silent. He looks on shock-pried faces.
History, even, does not know what is meant.

You would feel that after so many centuries
God would give man to repent; yet he can kill
As Cain could, but with multitudinous will,
No farther advanced than in his ancient furies.

Was man made stupid to see his own stupidity?
Is God by definition indifferent, beyond us all?
Is the eternal truth man's fighting soul
Wherein the Beast ravens in its own avidity?

Of Van Wettering I speak, and Averill,
Names on a list, whose faces I do not recall
But they are gone to early death, who late in school
Distinguished the belt feed lever from the belt holding pawl.

The Raid

They came out of the sun undetected,
Who had lain in the thin ships
All night long on the cold ocean,
Watched Vega down, the Wain hover,
Drank in the weakening dawn their brew,
And sent the lumbering death-laden birds
Level along the decks.

They came out of the sun with their guns geared,
Saw the soft and easy shape of that island
Laid on the sea,
An unwakening woman,
Its deep hollows and its flowing folds
Veiled in the garlands of its morning mists.
Each of them held in his aching eyes the erotic image,
And then tipped down,
In the target's trance,
In the ageless instant of the long descent,
And saw sweet chaos blossom below,
And felt in that flower the years release.

The perfect achievement.
They went back toward the sun crazy with joy,
Like wild birds weaving,
Drunkenly stunting;
Passed out over edge of that injured island,
Sought the rendezvous on the open sea
Where the ships would be waiting.

None were there.
Neither smoke nor smudge;
Neither spar nor splice nor rolling raft.
Only the wide waiting waste,
That each of them saw with intenser sight
Than he ever had spared it,
Who circled that spot,
The spent gauge caught in its final flutter,
And straggled down on their wavering wings
From the vast sky,
From the endless spaces,
Down at last for the low hover,
And the short quick quench of the sea.

Homeric Simile

As when a heavy bomber in the cloud
Having made some minutes good an unknown track;
Although the dead-reckoner triangulates
Departure and the stations he can fix,
Counting the thinness of the chilly air,
The winds aloft, the readings of the clocks;
And the radarman sees the green snakes dance
Continually before him in attest
That the hostile sought terrain runs on below;
And although the phantom shapes of friendly planes
Flit on the screen and sometimes through the cloud
Where the pilot squints against the forward glass,
Seeing reflected phosphorescent dials
And his own anxious face in all command;
And each man thinks of some unlikely love,
Hitherto his; and issues drop away
Like jettisoned bombs, and all is personal fog;
Then, hope aside and hunger all at large
For certainty what war is, foe is, where America;
Then, the four engines droning like a sorrow,
Clear, sudden miracle: cloud breaks,
Tatter of cloud passes, there ahead,
Beside, above, friends in the desperate sky;
And below burns like all fire the target town,
A delicate red chart of squares, abstract
And jewelled, from which rise lazy tracers,
And the searchlights through smoke tumble up
To a lovely apex on some undone friend;
As in this fierce discovery is something found
More than release from waiting or of bombs,
Greater than all the Germanies of hate,

Some penetration of the overcast
We make through, hour upon uncounted hour,
All this life, fuel low, instruments all tumbled,
And uncrewed.

　　　　　Not otherwise the closing notes disclose,
As the calm, intelligent strings do their duty,
The hard objective of a quartet, reached
After uncertain passage, through form observed,
And at a risk no particle diminished.

The Death of the Ball Turret Gunner

From my mother's sleep I fell into the State,
And I hunched in its belly till my wet fur froze.
Six miles from earth, loosed from its dream of life,
I woke to black flak and the nightmare fighters.
When I died they washed me out of the turret with a hose.

Losses

It was not dying: everybody died.
It was not dying: we had died before
In the routine crashes—and our fields
Called up the papers, wrote home to our folks,
And the rates rose, all because of us.
We died on the wrong page of the almanac,
Scattered on mountains fifty miles away;
Diving on haystacks, fighting with a friend,
We blazed up on the lines we never saw.
We died like aunts or pets or foreigners.
(When we left high school nothing else had died
For us to figure we had died like.)

In our new planes, with our new crews, we bombed
The ranges by the desert or the shore,
Fired at towed targets, waited for our scores—
And turned into replacements and woke up
One morning, over England, operational.
It wasn't different: but if we died
It was not an accident but a mistake
(But an easy one for anyone to make).
We read our mail and counted up our missions—
In bombers named for girls, we burned
The cities we had learned about in school—
Till our lives wore out; our bodies lay among
The people we had killed and never seen.
When we lasted long enough they gave us medals;
When we died they said, "Our casualties were low."
They said, "Here are the maps"; we burned the cities.

It was not dying—no, not ever dying;
But the night I died I dreamed that I was dead,
And the cities said to me: "Why are you dying?
We are satisfied, if you are; but why did I die?"

Tuskegee Airfield

for the Tuskegee Airmen

These men,
these proud black men:
our first to touch
their fingers to the sky.

The Germans learned to call them
Die Schwarzen Vogelmenschen.
They called themselves
The Spookwaffe.

Laughing.
And marching to class under officers
whose thin-lipped ambition
was to *wash the niggers out.*

Sitting at attention
for lectures about ailerons, airspeed, altimeters
from boring lieutenants who believed
you monkeys ain't meant to fly.

Oh, there were parties,
cadet-dances, guest appearances
by the Count
and the lovely Lena.

There was the embarrassing
adulation of Negro civilians.
A woman approached my father in a bar

where he was drinking with his buddies.
Hello, Airman. She held out her palm.
Will you tell me my future?

There was that,
like a breath of pure oxygen.
But first
they had to earn wings.

There was this one instructor
who was pretty nice.
I mean, we just sat around
and *talked* when a flight had gone well.

But he was from Minnesota,
and he made us sing
the Minnesota Fight Song
before we took off.

If you didn't sing it,
your days were numbered.
"Minnesota, hats off to thee . . ."
That bastard!

One time I had a check-flight
with an instructor from Louisiana.
As we were about to head for base,
he chopped the power.

Force-landing, nigger.
There were trees everywhere I looked.
Except on that little island . . .
I began my approach.

The instructor said, *Pull Up.*
That was an excellent approach.
Real surprised.
But where would you have taken off, wise guy?

I said, *Sir,*
I was ordered
to land the plane.
Not take off.

The instructor grinned.
Boy, if your ass
is as hard as your head,
you'll go far in this world.

V-J Day

On the tallest day in time, the dead came back.
Clouds met us in the pastures past a world.
By short wave the releases of a rack
Exploded on the interphone's new word.

Halfway past Iwo we jettisoned to sea
Our gift of bombs like tears and tears like bombs
To spring a frolic fountain daintily
Out of the blue metallic seas of doom.

No fire-shot cloud pursued us going home.
No cities cringed and wallowed in the flame.
Far out to sea a blank millennium
Changed us alive, and left us still the same.

Lightened, we banked like jays, antennae squawking.
The four wild metal halos of our props
Blurred into time. The interphone was talking
Abracadabra to the cumulus tops:

Dreamboat three-one to Yearsend—loud and clear,
Angels one-two, on course at one-six-nine.
Magellan to Balboa. Propwash to Century.
How do you read me? Bombay to Valentine.

Fading and out. And all the dead were homing.
(*Wisecrack to Halfmast. Doom to Memory.*)
On the tallest day in time we saw them coming,
Wheels jammed and flaming on a metal sea.

The War in the Air

For a saving grace, we didn't see our dead,
Who rarely bothered coming home to die
But simply stayed away out there
In the clean war, the war in the air.

Seldom the ghosts came back bearing their tales
Of hitting the earth, the incompressible sea,
But stayed up there in the relative wind,
Shades fading in the mind,

Who had no graves but only epitaphs
Where never so many spoke for never so few:
Per ardua, said the partisans of Mars,
Per aspera, to the stars.

That was the good war, the war we won
As if there were no death, for goodness' sake,
With the help of the losers we left out there
In the air, in the empty air.

The Aging Poet, on a Reading Trip to Dayton, Visits the Air Force Museum and Discovers There a Plane He Once Flew

There was in danger desperate delight
When I in that ship was a stowaway.
It was primitive, I its proselyte.

Remembering, I give myself a fright
And the plane a pat, which still is to say
There was in danger desperate delight.

Or is that now romantic second-sight?
Machined in deadly earnest, not for play,
It was primitive, I its proselyte.

But, oh, that detachment, that impolite
Aloofness when I was its protégé.
There was in danger desperate delight

Of high, blue pasture through which to excite
By joystick whip a racing runaway.
It was primitive, I its proselyte.

Grounded now, hangared here, she was my rite.
We are survivors to a duller day.
There was in danger desperate delight.
It was primitive, I its proselyte.

Thunderbirds

Spectators' murmur heralds them.
Our faces and eyes in unison
Front four small shapes
Massed in middle distance hanging
There framed a moment then
Like silent thought passing
Before us.
Stately parade! Four warplanes
Resplendent in bright ceremonial dress,
Streaming bold white smoke pennants,
Turbines calling throaty cadence as
One they pivot up
Commanding eyes which squint to see
Color poised balanced inverted
A moment against bright sky.

Brave spectacle! I suddenly remember another
Poised and balanced moment as I
Yank six or seven G's in a
Jolting Thunderbird in dull war paint
Shoving and pushing against
My craning neck and sweat stung eyes tearing
Me sluggishly up away from smoky jungle from
Which I apprehend
A solemn procession of
Bright
Red
Fireballs
Marching up
To some imagined apex.

Cobra Pilot

Plastic blue eyes
and hair
the color of toggle switches.
He flies his cobra-shark
with the precision
of a god
or a gunfighter.
(Hickok
with a 38 in his armpit)
His Nebraska smile
is a mini-gun
and his bowels
are full of rockets.
He hunts
the Indian-gooks
in the Wild West
of his mind

Air Field

All day the great planes gingerly descend
an invisible staircase, holding up
their skirts and dignity like great ladies
in technicolor histories, or reascend,
their noses needling upward like a compass
into a wild blue vacuum,
leaving everything in confusion behind:

In some such self-deceiving light as this
we'll view the air force base when moved away
from where its sleepless eye revolves all night.
We'll smile and recollect it conversationally—
tell with what ease the silver planes dropped down
or how they, weightless, rose above
our roof. We'll pass it with the sugar and cream,

forever sheltered from this moment's sick
surprise that we have lived with terror, with pride,
the wounded god circling the globe, never resting,
that in the morning and the evening we have heard
his cry, have seen him drag his silver wings
whining with anguish like a huge
fly seeking to lay its deadly eggs.

P. L. DELANO (1973)

Sonnet for an SR-71

The night is caught on the web of her wings
As fiery through the cold the black beast flies;
And faint and far the frosted starlight sings
The chill song of these ancient, empty skies—
She does not hear. Her many seeking eyes
Turn ever to the spinning world below—
Pattern of heat and cold to be allies
And tell to her the things that she must know
Of the city hid beneath the shadow
Of her sweeping wings; and the rushing air
Brings to her knowledge of the ebb and flow
Of hurried life; yet still she does not care.

The silent splendor of the high-borne dawn
Finds the sky untouched—and the black beast gone.

The War in Bosnia

Under darkness of stars our son flies
over Bosnia, keeping watch over snow.
Apache gunships will be out tonight.

The moon on foreign snowfields highlights
bodies running under trees, friend or foe.
Under darkness of stars our son flies

with star scope and rockets and wide eyes
over war zones bitter enemies know.
Apache gunships will be out tonight.

What keeps a nation armed and justifies
air power is such a killing field—we know,
but under darkness of stars our son flies.

In boots and parka, someone watches the skies
and owns disposable Stingers, and is cold.
Apache gunships will be out tonight.

I conjure God to stop him, warp his sights.
I stare with the prayer all fathers know.
Under darkness of stars our son flies.
Apache gunships will be out tonight.

PART FIVE

Icarus Falling

Grief travels toward you this way
out of the blue. It finds you
unprepared . . .
GARDNER MCFALL from "Moves" (1996)

This man escaped the dirty fates,
Knowing that he died nobly, as he died.

Darkness, nothingness of human after-death,
Receive and keep him in the deepnesses of space—

Profundum, physical thunder, dimension in which
We believe without belief, beyond belief.
WALLACE STEVENS "Flyer's Fall" (1947)

Landscape with the Fall of Icarus

According to Brueghel
when Icarus fell
it was spring

a farmer was ploughing
his field
the whole pageantry

of the year was
awake tingling
near

the edge of the sea
concerned
with itself

sweating in the sun
that melted
the wings' wax

unsignificantly
off the coast
there was

a splash quite unnoticed
this was
Icarus drowning

ANNE SEXTON (1962)

To a Friend Whose Work Has Come to Triumph

Consider Icarus, pasting those sticky wings on,
testing that strange little tug at his shoulder blade,
and think of that first flawless moment over the lawn
of the labyrinth. Think of the difference it made!
There below are the trees, as awkward as camels;
and here are the shocked starlings pumping past
and think of innocent Icarus who is doing quite well:
larger than a sail, over the fog and the blast
of the plushy ocean, he goes. Admire his wings!
Feel the fire at his neck and see how casually
he glances up and is caught, wondrously tunneling
into that hot eye. Who cares that he fell back to the sea?
See him acclaiming the sun and come plunging down
while his sensible daddy goes straight into town.

Icarus

Only the feathers floating around the hat
Showed that anything more spectacular had occurred
Than the usual drowning. The police preferred to ignore
The confusing aspects of the case,
And the witnesses ran off to a gang war.
So the report filed and forgotten in the archives read simply
"Drowned," but it was wrong: Icarus
Had swum away, coming at last to the city
Where he rented a house and tended the garden.

"That nice Mr. Hicks" the neighbors called him,
Never dreaming that the gray, respectable suit
Concealed arms that had controlled huge wings
Nor that those sad, defeated eyes had once
Compelled the sun. And had he told them
They would have answered with a shocked, uncomprehending
    stare.
No, he could not disturb their neat front yards;
Yet all his books insisted that this was a horrible mistake:
What was he doing aging in a suburb?
Can the genius of the hero fall
To the middling stature of the merely talented?

And nightly Icarus probes his wound
And daily in his workshop, curtains carefully drawn,
Constructs small wings and tries to fly
To the lighting fixture on the ceiling:
Fails every time and hates himself for trying.

He had thought himself a hero, had acted heroically,
And dreamt of his fall, the tragic fall of the hero;
But now rides commuter trains,
Serves on various committees,
And wishes he had drowned.

Ceiling Unlimited

III

The cattle-trains edge along the river, bringing morning on a
    white vibration
breaking the darkness split with beast-cries: a milk-wagon proceeds
down the street leaving the cold bottles: the Mack truck pushes
around the corner, tires hissing on the washed asphalt. A
    clear sky
growing candid and later bright.
                              Ceiling unlimited. Visibility unlimited.

They stir on the pillows, her leg moving, her face swung
    windowward
vacant with sleep still, modeled with light's coming; his dark head
among the softness of her arm and breast, nuzzled in dreams,
mumbling the old words, hardly roused. They return to
    silence.
                              At the airport, the floodlights are snapped off.

Turning, he says, "Tell me how's the sky this morning?" "Fair,"
    she answers,
"no clouds from where I lie; bluer and bluer." "And later
    and later—
god, for some sleep into some noon, instead of all these mornings
with my mouth going stiff behind the cowling and wind brushing
away from me and my teeth freezing against the wind."
                              Light gales from the northwest: tomorrow, rain.

The street is long, with a sprinkling of ashcans; panhandlers
begin to forage among banana-peels and cardboard boxes.
She moves to the window, tall and dark before a brightening sky,
full with her six-months' pregnancy molded in ripeness.
                    Stands, watching the sky's blankness.

Very soon: "How I love to see you when I wake," he says,
"How the child's meaning in you is my life's growing."
She faces him, hands brought to her belly's level, offering,
wordless, looking upon him. She carries his desire well.
                    Sun rises: 6:38 A.M. Sun sets. . . .

"Flying is what makes you strange to me, dark as Asia,
almost removed from my world even in your closenesses:
that you should be familiar with those intricacies
and a hero in mysteries which all the world has wanted."
                    Wind velocity changing from 19 to 30.

"No, that's wrong," and he laughs, "no personal hero's left
to make a legend. Those centuries have gone. If I fly,
why, I know that countries are not map-colored, that seas
belong to no one, that war's a pock-marking on Europe:"
                    The Weather Bureau's forecast, effective until noon.

"Your friends sleep with strange women desperately,
drink liquor and sleep heavily to forget those skies.
You fly all day and come home truly returning
to me who know only land. And we will have this child."
                    New York to Boston: Scattered to broken clouds.

"The child will have a hard time to be an American,"
he says slowly, "fathered by a man whose country is air,
who believes there are no heroes to withstand
wind, or a loose bolt, or a tank empty of gas."
                    To Washington: Broken clouds becoming overcast.

"It will be a brave child," she answers, smiling.
"We will show planes to it, and the bums in the street.
You will teach it to fly, and I will love it
very much." He thinks of his job, dressing.
                    Strong west northwest winds above 1000 feet.

He thinks how many men have wanted flight.
He ties his tie, looking into his face.
Finishes breakfast, hurrying to be gone,
crossing the river to the airport and his place.
                    To Cleveland: Broken clouds to overcast.

She does not imagine how the propeller turns
in a blinding speed, swinging the plane through space;
she never sees the cowling rattle and slip
forward and forward against the grim blades' grinding.
                    Cruising speed 1700 R.P.M.

Slipping, a failing desire; slipping like death
insidious against the propeller, until the blades shake,
bitten by steel, jagged against steel, broken,
and his face angry and raked by death, staring.
                    Strong west northwest or west winds above 2000 feet.

She watches the clock as his return time hurries,
the schedule ticking off, eating the short minutes.
She watches evening advance; she knows the child's stirring.
She knows night. She knows he will not come.
                    Ceiling unlimited. Visibility unlimited.

The Old Pilot

He discovers himself on an old airfield.
He thinks he was there before,
but rain has washed out the lettering of a sign.
A single biplane, all struts and wires,
stands in the long grass and wildflowers.
He pulls himself into the narrow cockpit
although his muscles are stiff
and sits like an egg in a nest of canvas.
He sees that the machine gun has rusted.
The glass over the instruments
has broken, and the red arrows are gone
from his gas gauge and his altimeter.
When he looks up, his propeller is turning,
although no one was there to snap it.
He lets out the throttle. The engine catches
and the propeller spins into the wind.
He bumps over holes in the grass,
and he remembers to pull back on the stick.
He rises from the land in a high bounce
which gets higher, and suddenly he is flying again.
He feels the old fear, and rising over the fields
the old gratitude. In the distance, circling
in a beam of late sun like birds migrating,
there are the wings of a thousand biplanes.

The Lost Pilot

for my father, 1922–1944

Your face did not rot
like the others—the co-pilot,
for example, I saw him

yesterday. His face is corn-
mush: his wife and daughter,
the poor ignorant people, stare

as if he will compose soon.
He was more wronged than Job.
But your face did not rot

like the others—it grew dark,
and hard like ebony;
the features progressed in their

distinction. If I could cajole
you to come back for an evening,
down from your compulsive

orbiting, I would touch you,
read your face as Dallas,
your hoodlum gunner, now,

with the blistered eyes, reads
his braille editions. I would
touch your face as a disinterested

scholar touches an original page.
However frightening, I would
discover you, and I would not

turn you in; I would not make
you face your wife, or Dallas,
or the co-pilot, Jim. You

could return to your crazy
orbiting, and I would not try
to fully understand what

it means to you. All I know
is this: when I see you,
as I have seen you at least

once every year of my life,
spin across the wilds of the sky
like a tiny, African god,

I feel dead. I feel as if I were
the residue of a stranger's life,
that I should pursue you.

My head cocked toward the sky,
I cannot get off the ground,
and, you, passing over again,

fast, perfect, and unwilling
to tell me that you are doing
well, or that it was mistake

that placed you in that world,
and me in this; or that misfortune
placed these worlds in us.

The Airman

He laughed at death,
Pursued him with a kiss
Climbed to the skies
Pursued him to a star
But death, who never had
Been wooed like this,
Remained aloof, afar

With spurt and gleam and
Brightness like the sun's
He circled death as with a
Wheel of flame
But death, capricious,
Sought those other ones
Who had not called his name

He mocked at death
Pursued him into hell
Mocked him afresh, then
Crashed to burning space
But death, grown gentle,
Caught him as he fell
Nor let him see his face.

Missing

For years I lived with the thought
of his return. I imagined he had ditched
the plane and was living on a distant
island, plotting his way back
with a faithful guide; or, if
he didn't have a guide, he was sending
up a flare in sight of an approaching ship.

Perhaps, having reached an Asian capital,
he was buying gifts for a reunion
that would dwarf the ones before.
He would have exotic stories to tell,
though after a while, the stories
didn't matter or the gifts.

One day I told myself, he is not coming
home, though I had no evidence,
no grave, nothing to say a prayer over.
I knew he was flying among the starry
plankton, detained forever.
But telling myself this was as futile
as when I found a picture of him

sleeping in the ready room,
hands folded across his chest,
exhausted from the sortie he'd flown.
His flight suit was still on,
a jacket collapsed at his feet.
I half thought I could reach out

and wake him, as the unconscious
touches the object of its desire
and makes it live. I have kept
all the doors open in my life
so that he could walk in, unsure
as I've been how to relinquish
what is not there.

DONALD HALL (1969)

The Man in the Dead Machine

High on a slope in New Guinea
the Grumman Hellcat
lodges among bright vines
as thick as arms. In nineteen-forty-three,
the clenched hand of a pilot
glided it here
where no one has ever been.

In the cockpit the helmeted
skeleton sits
upright, held
by dry sinews at neck
and shoulder, and by webbing
that straps the pelvic cross
to the cracked
leather of the seat, and the breastbone
to the canvas cover
of the parachute.

Or say that the shrapnel
missed me, I flew
back to the carrier, and every morning
take the train, my pale
hands on a black case, and sit
upright, held
by the firm webbing.

Waiting for Icarus

He said he would be back and we'd drink wine together
He said that everything would be better than before
He said we were on the edge of a new relation
He said he would never again cringe before his father
He said that he was going to invent full-time
He said he loved me that going into me
He said was going into the world and the sky
He said all the buckles were very firm
He said the wax was the best wax
He said Wait for me here on the beach
He said Just don't cry

I remember the gulls and the waves
I remember the islands going dark on the sea
I remember the girls laughing
I remember they said he only wanted to get away from me
I remember mother saying   :   Inventors are like poets,
                                                a trashy lot
I remember she told me those who try out inventions are worse
I remember she added   :   Women who love such are the
    worst of all
I have been waiting all day, or perhaps longer.
I would have liked to try those wings myself.
It would have been better than this.

In Flight

The Whisperjet swings wildly
From one air pocket to another
As I fly to bury you.

Is it you, jostling the plane,
Making sure you have the last word?

We dip into shadow. I feel
Your loss as if my own vital signs
Were failing. The plane steadies.
Light floods the window.

I search the sky for something
Familiar, a Sunday School scene
Colored too bright, a figure
Soaring against all gravity and sense

And think I see you rise
From a white cloud that spirals
Off the tail—my brother
Leaping like a boy who believes

He can fly. One arm beckons,
The other is beating like a wing.

The Black Hole

Imagine [that] the whole mass of the sun is crushed down to a radius of a few kilometers. The gravity and space curvature near this compacted sun is enormous. If a light beam were sent out to hit and bounce off this object, it would never return. . . . Since light cannot leave this object, it "appears" as a black hole in space. . . . An observer who fell into the center of a black hole could see time slow down. But the falling observer can never communicate his strange experience to his friend outside.
HEINZ R. PAGELS, Perfect Symmetry

My brother and I planned to meet
at our secluded campsite up in Maine
         beside an azure lake
swarming with rainbow trout. I'd hired a local plane

    to fly me to our dock, but when
I saw how beaten up it was, how queerly
       the old pilot squinted upwind
at the sun, I felt a fleeting shock of fear.

    A reject of the Wright Brothers?
Or had he built it with his son—sort of
       a modern Daedalus?
Its banged pontoons were dented right above

    the water line which seemed to me
too high for the sad bird to lift its ass
       for takeoff. But, by God,
it did! The pilot made, I thought, a needless pass

between two quarry walls,
then brushed the treetops just to show
where a tornado scythed
a highway through the woods, ten years ago,

which wound back on itself.
When we arrived, my waiting brother waved his hands
wildly from the dock's edge.
The pilot asked, "How's 'bout before we land

we do a couple lucky loops?"
The first loop made me squeeze
my thighs against my groin, and with the second,
wider loop, the engine wheezed,

shuddered and stopped. We slid into a nosedive,
spinning toward the evening sun
reflected in the lake. Oh, I was falling
through my mind's black hole, the one

curved space to float me home,
so slowly I had time to think that I
alone had nothing left to know
except the circle of the sun within the sky

inside the water, blue advancing
bluer into brighter blue—
although my unbelieving brother held his hands
over his face. And you,

Professor Pagels, would you not have seen,
reflected in my eyes,
the unresisted pull into the perfect heart
of orange light, the last surprise

of pure acceptance that can never pass
                         beyond itself? I guess
    the gas ran back into the engine,
                         for we leveled out, and, yes,

    terror returned the instant we touched down,
                         and my taut body knew
    that I was safe there in my brother's arms.
                         Next morning my whole chest was bruised

    where I had clutched myself, and one week later,
                         back in the old river town
    by the abandoned mill, we learned my pilot's plane
                         had crashed in the dense mountain

    flying home. "Don't know how Joel lasted
                         long's he did," his neighbor said.
    We sat, a covenant of brothers by the fire,
                         and yet the orange-red,

    the green-blue flames distracted me; I watched
                         the sizzling rainbow trout that night,
    its smeared red stripe surrounded by black dots—
                         collapsed suns lost in their trapped light.

Black Box

Because the cockpit, like the snowy village in a paperweight,
parodies the undomed world outside, and because
even a randomly composed society like Air Florida

flight #7 needs minutes for its meeting, the tape
in the black box slithers and loops with its slow,
urinary hiss like the air-filtering system in a fall-

out shelter. What's normally on the tape? Office life
at 39,000 feet, radio sputter and blab, language
on automatic pilot. Suppose the flight should fail.

Cosseted against impact and armored against fire,
the black box records not time but history. Bad choice.
The most frequent last word on the black box

tape is "Mother." Will this change if we get
more female pilots? Who knows? But here's
the best exchange: "We're going down." "I know."

SAM HAMOD (1980, REVISED 2004)

Libyan Airliner/Egyptian Acrobats/Israeli Air Circus

February 21, 1973

the fighters come
from the left of the plane
I can see them   they are to my right
I see them
they slant in from the left behind the tail
the first Phantom streaks in at 45 degrees
he's at 8 o'clock when he lets loose
his rockets flash forward
bang into the wing tank
wing explodes
it comes apart s l o w l y i n t h e a i r ,
suddenly
another explosion   the plane
is coming apart,
the people, so small in the large sky
are performing acrobatics,
they tumble
carelessly through the sky
as if they are performing for the Israeli Air Circus,
these dolls' arms come off as the planes strafe,
the French pilot in the Libyan airliner is the only one
who can see where he's going,
he's going down,
down   down
into the hardness of scrabble desert rock and sand;
there is no Hebrew parallelism here,
these are not simply eyes you take

CHARLES MUÑOZ (1994)

Lockerbie

I have never understood
how Zeno's famous paradox could twist
through anybody's mind
without damaging
a few brain cells, scorching them with sparks from that brilliant

absurdity of never-ending travel. When the airplane had spun
halfway down from eight miles up, it still, naturally,
had half of the original eight
miles left to go,
a four-mile cushion of clear air and of reasonable safety as long

as it stayed in the sky, and, continuing to obey
that law of demi-
proportionality, it could spin its passengers halfway down the sky
again, a precise half of those four cushioning
miles, which would leave, as always, another

half of the distance
safely remaining, so now there would be two miles of air below
each passenger's pressing
feet, an altitude
then to be divided into equal segments by tumbled gyro

compass and hazy straightedge
horizon, though, to tell the truth, the controls had lost all function.
Zeno was, at that next moment,
one full mile from harm (philosophers die old), and he easily
fell halfway yet again,

teaching that no matter how far you travel
from that last bed,
you can always split
the difference
and find yourself a chunk of time useful for thinking and
    falling, but

by then even Zeno was only a half
mile above the town's scrubby trees, the village where faces
had already started to look
up. From a quarter mile above
the streets you could glance down

and see one arm pointing at you, see mouths crying
"O," see faces, mouths and eyes defining
well-constructed geometric circles,
see town turning as the plane spun, radius and
diameter shown to all of us, see the whole great wheel

of the universe and the irrational
number shaped by the wingtips,
and you could surely feel the discipline
of centrifugal force
that kept the passengers securely clenched

to cushions whose upholstery
springs popped upward through the plastic seats,
heads pulled back so
hard that mouths
dragged open, eyes

watching black shadows in the sunlight that flashed into alternate
windows of the broken cabin, as round they went,
drawing geometry
in the sky, pinned, held fast by that spinning gravitation, clutched
by the simple physics that shoved

their magazines and underseat
baggage against the sides of the airplane and filled
flickering space with dust. They heard the loudspeaker sizzling, saw
the perfect circles of their coffee cups, felt
time disturbed

by granite hills, space wrenched
by roof tiles, and they believed
Zeno's elegant demonstration that never will we get
to that last point of our travels
(nor fly into the sun),

not even when the town's sheep meadow, upside down, spins
over us. For still there will be time
for a wind of treetops,
weeds between the trees,
and a space of white rocks.

The Women of Lockerbie

After the explosion and the hail
of fire and linen, after hot steel
cooled on the ground, they buried each neighbor
or son, undertook the terrible

reunion that began with quiet heaps
of travelers' clothing left on each stoop
by the coroner. In their own kitchens
they picked bits of hair, bone from the slope

of a shoulder yoke, they bleached out soot,
perfume of fear, their tired Scottish dirt
before they washed the clothes for a last time,
dried them on a line in west wind, brought

each thing back inside for the pressing,
the folding, the packing in tissue
before all was sent back in parcels
marked for shipping to the grieved ends of earth.

Above the City

You know our office on the 18th
floor of the Salmon Tower looks
    right out on the

Empire State and it just happened
we were there finishing up some
    late invoices on

a new book that Saturday morning
when a bomber roared through the
    mist and crashed

flames poured from the windows
into the drifting clouds and sirens
    screamed down in

the streets below   it was unearthly
but you know the strangest thing
    we realized that

none of us had been surprised be-
cause we'd always known that those
    two Paragons of

progress sooner or later would demonstrate
before our eyes their true
    relationship

History of the Airplane

And the Wright brothers said they thought they had invented
something that could make peace on earth (if the wrong
    brothers didn't
get hold of it) when their wonderful flying machine took off at
    Kitty Hawk
into the kingdom of birds but the parliament of birds was
    freaked out
by this man-made bird and fled to heaven

And then the famous Spirit of Saint Louis took off eastward and
flew across the Big Pond with Lindy at the controls in his leather
helmet and goggles hoping to sight the doves of peace but he
    did not
Even though he circled Versailles

And then the famous Flying Clipper took off in the opposite
direction and flew across the terrific Pacific but the pacific doves
were frighted by this strange amphibious bird and hid in the
    orient sky

And then the famous Flying Fortress took off bristling with guns
and testosterone to make the world safe for peace and capitalism
but the birds of peace were nowhere to be found before or after
    Hiroshima

And so then clever men built bigger and faster flying machines and
these great man-made birds with jet plumage flew higher than
    any
real birds and seemed about to fly into the sun and melt their
    wings
and like Icarus crash to earth

And the Wright brothers were long forgotten in the high-flying
bombers that now began to visit their blessings on various Third
Worlds all the while claiming they were searching for doves of
peace

And they kept flying and flying until they flew right into the 21st
century and then one fine day a Third World struck back and
stormed the great planes and flew them straight into the beating
heart of Skyscraper America where there were no aviaries and no
parliaments of doves and in a blinding flash America became
   a part
of the scorched earth of the world

And a wind of ashes blows across the land
And for one long moment in eternity
There is chaos and despair

And buried loves and voices
Cries and whispers
Fill the air
Everywhere

PART SIX

Space Odysseys

First a monkey, then a man.
Just the way the world began.
JOHN CIARDI "Dawn of the Space Age" (1962)

The astronauts. . . . In a sense they are all poets, expanders of
consciousness beyond its known limits. Because of them, the
death-cold and blazing craters of the moon will think with us,
and the waterless oceans of Mars; the glowing fogs of Venus will
say what they are.
    And those places will change us also. We have not
lived them yet, and perhaps have no language adequate to them.
But these men will find that, too . . .
JAMES DICKEY from "A Poet Witnesses a Bold Mission" (1968)

first Apollo's blaze,
    now your grand fire, lightning
        bug in moonflower
RAYMOND ROSELIEP "Night of Lift-Off 7.16.69" (1970)

Cold stones jumbled in a heap.
Lifeless plains, sharing only the sun
With a verdant recollection I must keep . . .
MICHAEL COLLINS from "Ode to the Moon's Far Side" (1974)

Earth's Bondman

When man has conquered space
What will be his gain?
The moon's pocked face
Unmollified by rain,

The far cold reaches
Between star and star,
The blast-carved beaches
Where no seas are

Nor any wind sings
Nor any gull cries;
Where no herb springs
Nor germinates nor dies?

Though the universe be his,
The last void spanned,
Not all the galaxies
Can break his ancient bond

With cloud and leaf and sod.
The earth is in his flesh,
The tide is in his blood;
So intricate the mesh

That moors him to his star.
Adventurer by will,
By nature insular,
He wears Earth's livery still.

Dog Asleep

Dogs have dreams of Laika, her free soul,
her spaced heartbeat that radioed, "We're lost!"
Dogs twitch their feet.

We tell some point in space, "It's for the best,
and Laika volunteered—she wagged her tail."
We twitch our feet.

Heel & Toe to the End

Gagarin says, in ecstasy,
he could have
gone on forever

he floated
ate and sang
and when he emerged from that

one hundred eight minutes off
the surface of
the earth he was smiling

Then he returned
to take his place
among the rest of us

from all that division and
subtraction a measure
toe and heel

heel and toe he felt
as if he had
been dancing

The Crew of *Apollo 8*

Shall we call them poets, for having observed
on their earliest times around
the moon that it seemed to be
layered with
a grayish white beach sand
with footprints in it? Or geologists
for having reported to us
the six or seven terraces leading
down
into crater Langrenus?

Or shall we call them some new
breed of bird
for having swiftly flown
weightless and unfearing and
sharp-eyed
into the dark unknown?
Yet words to tell of their skill and
valiancy
are as weak as water—
and their return, and being earthlings
with us
again, are what most matter.

Countdown

T minus 60 seconds
and counting
marbles on 4th Street
which Joey collected
since age 5½
years ago the
buildings were new
but now they're
falling down
to T minus 50
on the Cape
and all systems are go
up the street
to Stuyvesant which
is the end of the
world and beyond
it are monsters breathing
jet propulsion fuel
now disconnected from
the pad at T minus 40
all systems are green
light at the corner
by the delicatessen
where meat is grown
in white wax-paper
and milk is made in
bottles like the ones
Daddy brings home to the
pad now cleared at
T minus 30 while voice
communications with

the world through the
welfare worker are not
proceeding at T minus
20 and now removed
from the launching room
are 2 dead rats and
Mammy is screaming
10, 9, 8, 7 days till
the next check comes for
6, 5, 4, 3 dollars or even
2, 1, Zero, Ignition, Lift-Off
to buy a pair of brand
new shining rockets.

A Farewell, a Welcome

After the lunar landings

Good-bye pale cold inconstant
tease, you never existed
therefore we had to invent you

    Good-bye crooked little man
    huntress who sleeps alone
    dear pastor, shepherd of stars
    who tucked us in   Good-bye

Good riddance phony prop
con man moon
who tap-danced with June
to the tender surrender
of love from above

Good-bye decanter of magic liquids
fortuneteller *par excellence*
seducer   incubus   medicine man
exile's sanity   love's sealed lips
womb that nourished the monstrous child
and the sweet ripe grain   Good-bye
    We trade you in as we traded
    the evil eye for the virus
    the rosy seat of affections
    for the indispensable pump
we say good-bye as we said good-bye
to angels in nightgowns   to Grandfather God

Good-bye forever Edam and Gorgonzola
cantaloupe in the sky
night watchman, one-eyed loner
wolves nevertheless
are programmed to howl   Good-bye
        forbidden lover good-bye
        sleepwalkers will wander
        with outstretched arms for no reason
        while you continue routinely
        to husband the sea, prevail
        in the fix of infant strabismus
Good-bye ripe ovum   women will spill their blood
in spite of you now   lunatics wave good-bye
accepting despair by another name

Welcome new world to the brave old words
Peace   Hope   Justice
Truth Everlasting   welcome
ash-colored playground of children
happy in airy bags
never to touch is never to miss it

Scarface hello   we've got you covered
welcome untouchable   outlaw
with an alias in every country
salvos and roses   you are home
our footprints stamp you mortal

BABETTE DEUTSCH (1970)

To the Moon, 1969

You are not looked for through the smog, you turn blindly
Behind that half palpable poison—you who no longer
Own a dark side, yet whose radiance falters, as if it were fading.
Now you have been reached, you are altered
                                        beyond belief—
As a stranger spoken to, remaining remote, changes from
    being a stranger.
Astronomers know you a governor of tides, women as the
    mistress
Of menstrual rhythms, poets have called you Hecate,
    Astarte, Artemis—huntress whose arrows
Fuse into a melt of moonlight as they pour
                                    upon earth, upon water.
We all know you a danger
    to the thief in the garden, the pilot
In the enemy plane, to lovers embraced in your promise
    of a shining security. Are you a monster?
A noble being? Or simply a planet that men have,
    almost casually, cheapened?
The heavens do not answer.
Once, it was said, the cry: "Pan is dead! Great Pan is dead!"
    shivered, howled, through the forests: the gentle
Christ had killed him.
There is no lament for you—who are silent
    as the dead always are.
You have left the mythologies, the old ones, our own.
But, for a few, what has happened is the death of a divine
    Person, is a betrayal, is a piece of
The cruelty that the Universe is witness to
                                while displaying its glories.

The Flight of Apollo

I

Earth was my home, but even there I was a stranger. This
mineral crust. I walk like a swimmer. What titanic bombardments
in those old astral wars! I know what I know: I shall never
escape from strangeness or complete my journey. Think of me
as nostalgic, afraid, exalted. I am your man on the moon, a speck
of megalomania, restless for the leap towards island universes
pulsing beyond where the constellations set. Infinite space
overwhelms the human heart, but in the middle of nowhere life
inexorably calls to life. Forward my mail to Mars. What news
from the Great Spiral Nebula in Andromeda and the Magellanic
Clouds?

II

I was a stranger on earth.
Stepping on the moon, I begin
the gay pilgrimage to new
Jerusalems
in foreign galaxies.
Heat. Cold. Craters of silence.
The Sea of Tranquility
rolling on the shores of entropy.
And, beyond,
the intelligence of the stars.

Voyage to the Moon

Wanderer in our skies,
dazzle of silver in our leaves and on our
waters silver, O
silver evasion in our farthest thought—
"the visiting moon," "the glimpses of the moon,"

and we have found her.

From the first of time,
before the first of time, before the
first men tasted time, we sought for her.
She was a wonder to us, unattainable,
a longing past the reach of longing,
a light beyond our lights, our lives—perhaps
a meaning to us—O, a meaning!

Now we have found her in her nest of night.

Three days and three nights we journeyed,
steered by farthest stars, climbed outward,
crossed the invisible tide-rip where the floating dust
falls one way or the other in the void between,
followed that other down, encountered
cold, faced death, unfathomable emptiness.

Now, the fourth day evening, we descend,
make fast, set foot at last upon her beaches,
stand in her silence, lift our heads and see
above her, wanderer in her sky,

a wonder to us past the reach of wonder,
a light beyond our lights, our lives, the rising
earth,
       a meaning to us,
              O, a meaning!

Walk on the Moon

for Henry Raymont
21 July 1969

Extend, there where you venture and come back,
The edge of Time. Be it your farthest track.
Time in that distance wanes. What is *to be*,
That present verb, there in Tranquility?

from Apollo

II: THE MOON GROUND

You look as though
You know me, though the world we came from is striking
You in the forehead like Apollo. Buddy,
We have brought the gods. We know what it is to shine
Far off, with earth. We alone
Of all men, could take off
Our shoes and fly. One-sixth of ourselves, we have gathered,
Both of us, under another one
Of us overhead. He is reading the dials he is understanding
Time, to save our lives. You and I are in earth
light and deep moon
shadow on magic ground
Of the dead new world, and we do not but we could
Leap over each other, like children in the universal playground
of stones
but we must not play
At being here: we must look
We must look for it: the stones are going to tell us
Not the why but the how of all things. Brother, your gold face flashes
On me. It is the earth. I hear your deep voice rumbling from the body
Of its huge clothes   Why did we come here
It does not say, but the ground looms, and the secret
Of time is lying
Within amazing reach. It is everywhere
We walk, our glass heads shimmering with absolute heat
And cold. We leap slowly
Along it. We will take back the very stones
Of Time, and build it where we live. Or in the cloud
striped blue of home, will the secret crumble

In our hands with air? Will the moon-plague kill our children
In their beds? The Human Planet trembles in its black
Sky with what we do   I can see it hanging in the god-gold only
Brother of your face. We are this world: we are
The only men. What hope is there at home
In the azure of breath, or here with the stone
Dead secret? My massive clothes bubble around me
Crackling with static and Gray's
Elegy helplessly coming
From my heart, and I say I think something
From high school I remember Now
Fades the glimmering landscape on the sight, and all the air
A solemn stillness holds. Earth glimmers
And in its air-color a solemn stillness holds
It. O brother! Earth-faced god! APOLLO! My eyes blind
With unreachable tears   my breath goes all over
Me and cannot escape. We are here to do one
Thing only, and that is rock by rock to carry the moon to take it
Back. Our clothes embrace we cannot touch we cannot
Kneel. We stare into the moon
dust, the earth-blazing ground. We laugh, with the beautiful craze
Of static. We bend, we pick up stones.

EVA Psalm

I

The old white beard of God is blowing
on the moon,
Old Glory shivers on a winter clothesline,
a spider eagle dozes in the dust.
Two dancers dance:
Tender ghosts of twinned Nureyev,

tipsy on the straight-up legbeat
puffing halos out of cocoa grit,
gamboling colts in dreamtime motion,
Keystone cops a little fat,
kangaroos in water mirror
landing softshoe as the cat:
their feet keep falling free.

II

Shadow heads Omega-point.
Light is flowing like a beard.

III

I-Thou.
We're on the moon.
Aye, Thou.

IV

Praise order, Jack-be-nimble,
praise *one small step*, Jack-man,
poke at the going embers of my life.
Hunt myself, Jack-hunter,
face up, Me-occupied.
Jubal, where's a harp, an organ?
Hang on a twig of language:
To that dance!

V

Ring.

Ring around those fat thieves
gathering up the moon,
run the keyboard of my ribs,
Jack! roll the wick still higher.
Shake the earth grain guilty
from each wrinkled sole,
jump your blood past limbo
of restricted birds.

Spring, dodge, spin,
wheel, loop, ride.
Fly inside.

VI

The old white beard of God
is dancing on the moon.

Annie Pearl Smith Discovers Moonlight

My mother, the sage of Aliceville, Alabama,
didn't believe that men had landed on the moon.
"They can do anything with cameras,"
she hissed to anyone and everyone who'd listen,
even as moonrock crackled
beneath Neil Armstrong's puffed boot.
While the gritty film spun and rewound and we
heard the snarled static of "One small step,"
my mother pouted and sniffed
and slammed skillets into the sink.
She was not impressed.
After all, it was 1969, a year fat with deceit.
So many miracles
had proven mere staging for lesser dramas.

But why this elaborate prank
staged in a desert "somewhere out west,"
where she insisted the cosmic gag unfolded?
"They are trying to fool us."
No one argued, since she seemed near tears,
remembering the nervy deceptions of her own skin—
mirrors that swallowed too much,
men who blessed her with touch only as warning.
A woman reduced to juices, sensation and ritual,
my mother saw the stars only as signals for sleep.
She had already been promised the moon.

And heaven too. Somewhere above her head
she imagined bubble-cheeked cherubs
lining the one and only road to salvation,
angels with porcelain faces and celestial choirs

wailing gospel brown enough to warp the seams of paradise.
But for heaven to be real, it could not be kissed,
explored,
strolled upon
or crumbled in the hands of living men.
It could not be the 10 o'clock news,
the story above the fold,
the breathless garble of a radio "special report."

My mother had twisted her tired body into prayerful knots,
worked twenty years in a candy factory,
dipping wrinkled hands into vats of lumpy chocolate,
and counted out dollars with her thin, doubled vision,
so that a heavenly seat would be plumped for her coming.
Now the moon,
the promised land's brightest bauble,
crunched plainer than sidewalk beneath ordinary feet.
And her Lord just lettin' it happen.

"Ain't nobody mentioned God in all this," she muttered
over a hurried dinner of steamed collards and cornbread.
"That's how I know they ain't up there.
Them stars, them planets ain't ours to mess with.
The Lord woulda showed Hisself if them men
done punched a hole in my heaven."
Daddy kicked my foot beneath the table;
we nodded, we chewed, we swallowed.
Inside me, thrill unraveled;
I imagined my foot touching down on the jagged rock,
blessings moving like white light through my veins.

Annie Pearl Smith rose from sleep that night
and tilted her face full toward a violated paradise.
My father told me how she whispered in tongues,
how she ached for a sign
she wouldn't have to die to believe.

Now I watch her clicking like a clock toward deliverance,
and I tell her that heaven still glows wide and righteous
with a place waiting just for her,
fashioned long ago by that lumbering dance
of feet both human and holy.

Astronauts

Armored in oxygen,
    faceless in visors—
mirrormasks reflecting
    the mineral glare and
shadow of moonscape—
    they walk slowmotion
floatingly the lifeless
    dust of Taurus
Littrow. And Wow, they
    exclaim; oh boy, this is it.

    They sing, exulting
(though trained to be wary
    of "emotion and
philosophy"), breaking
    the calcined stillness
of once Absolute Otherwhere.

Risking edges, earthlings
    to whom only
their machines are friendly
    (and God's radar-
watching eye?), they
    labor at gathering
proof of hypothesis;
    in snowshine of sunlight
dangerous as radium
    probe detritus for clues.

    What is it we wish them
to find for us, as

we watch them on our
screens? They loom there
    heroic antiheroes,
smaller than myth and
    poignantly human.
Why are we troubled?
    What do we ask of these men?
What do we ask of ourselves?

Witnessing the Launch of the Shuttle *Atlantis*

So much of life in the world is waiting, that
This day was no exception, so we waited
All morning long and into the afternoon.
I spent some of the time remembering
Dante, who did the voyage in the mind
Alone, with no more nor heavier machinery
Than the ghost of a girl giving him guidance;

And wondered if much was lost to gain all this
New world of engine and energy, where dream
Translates into deed. But when the thing went up
It was indeed impressive, as if hell
Itself opened to send its emissary
In search of heaven or "the unpeopled world"
(thus Dante of doomed Ulysses) "behind the sun."

So much of life in the world is memory
That the moment of the happening itself—
So rich with noise and smoke and rising clear
To vanish at the limit of our vision
Into the light blue light of afternoon—
Appeared no more, against the void in aim,
Than the flare of a match in sunlight, quickly snuffed.

What yet may come of this? We cannot know.
Great things are promised, as the promised land
Promised to Moses that he would not see
But a distant sight of, though the children would.
The world is made of pictures of the world,
And the pictures change the world into another world
We cannot know, as we knew not this one.

Elegy for *Challenger*

Wind-walkers,
how we envied you

riding a golden plume
on a glitter-mad trajectory

to watch Earth roll
her blooming hips below

and scout the shores
of still unnamed seas.

You were the Balboas
we longed to be,

all star-spangled grin,
upbeat and eager,

a nation's cameo.
When the sun went out

and you blew into your shadow,
horrors clanged

like falling bells.

You orbit our thoughts now
as last we saw you:

boarding a shuttle bound
out of this world,

quivering with thrill,
deadset, but tingling

to pitch an outpost
in our wilderness of doubt,

and climb that old ladder
whose rungs lead only higher.

We still dream your dream,
though we taste your fire.

Viking

I did it.
Who would have thought
that such a hulk
of rivets and scraps
could cross a sea of space?
You named me for voyagers,
for men who ravaged harbor towns
content with seizing
their women and gold.

Cool were the hands
that made me. Few cheered
when I embarked in flame.
No one expects a golden bounty
at the end of my crossing.
A strange tide carried me
weighted, then weightless,
then tugged to ground again,
devoid of passenger
and pilotless,
not even a goddess
carved on my prow.

Little was left of me
when I touched down in sand.
I did it,
before the alien hordes you dreamt of
could launch *their* fleet,
I touched this desolate
and long deserted ground.

Well earned, the name
you gave me. I dared
your greatest dream and won.
Salute me, my maker:
I invaded Mars.

Firmament on High

Once, we loved our sister satellite.
Desert Endymions hot to shoot off
we fashioned Cadillacs of ascent
to touch her dry Sea of Serenity.

What we thought heroic, wasn't.
Our old moon, Sagan says, is "boring,"
like police photos of gelid bodies
icepicked in the heart or neck.

Mars is a nastier myth, but
more *heimisch* for some latter-day
atom-energized Voyager
to lay by, the better to fly by

and finally, beyond Pluto, settle among
Eocene forms not yet imagined,
not humdrum, resourceful as rodents,
"intelligent life" we fondly call it,

meaning, smart enough to welcome *us*
their destiny, but smarter than us too,
having no need for cinema, jails
or moving vans to find out what they are.

An Open Letter to *Voyager II*

Dear Voyager:
       This is to thank you for
The last twelve years, and wishing you, what's more,
Well in your new career in vacant space.
When you next brush a star, the human race
Will be a layer of old sediment,
A wrinkle of the primates, a misspent
Youth of some zoömorphs. But you, your frail
Insectoid form, will skim the sparkling vale
Of the void practically forever. As
The frictionless light-years and -epochs pass,
The rigid constellations Earth admires
Will shift and rearrange their twinkling fires.
No tipped antenna-dish will strain to hear
Your whispered news, nor poet call you dear.

Ere then, let me assure you you've been grand.
A little shaky at the outset, and
Arthritic in the swivel-joints, antique
In circuitry, virtually deaf, and weak
As a refrigerator bulb, you kept
Those picture postcards coming. Signals crept
To Pasadena; there they were enhanced
Until those planets clear as daylight danced.
The stripes and swirls of Jupiter's slow boil,
Its crazy moons—one cracked, one fried in oil,
One glazed with ice, and one too raw to eat,
Still bubbling with the juice of inner heat—
Arrived on our astonished monitors.
Then, following a station break of years,
Fat Saturn rode your feeble beam, and lo!—

Not corny as we feared, but Art Deco—
The hard-edge, Technicolor rings; they spin
At different speeds, are merely meters thin,
And cast a flash-bulb's shadows. Planet three
Was Uranus (accented solemnly,
By anchormen, on the first syllable,
Lest viewers think the "your" too personal):
A glassy globe of gas upon its side,
Its nine faint braided rings at last descried,
Its corkscrew-shaped magnetic passions bared,
Its pocked attendants digitized and aired.
Last loomed, against the Oort Cloud, blue Neptune,
Its counterrevolutionary moon,
Its wispy arcs of rings and whitish streaks
Of unpredicted tempests—thermal freaks,
As if an unused backyard swimming pool,
Remote from stirring sunlight, dark and cool
(Sub-sub-sub-freezing), chose to make a splash.
Displays of splendid waste, of rounded trash!
Your looping miles of guided drift brought home
How fruitless cosmic space would be to roam.
One awful ball succeeds another, none
Fit for a shred or breath of life. Our lone
Delightful, verdant orb was primed to cede
The H_2O and O and N we need.
Your survey, in its scrupulous depiction,
Purged from the solar system science fiction—
No more Uranians or Io-ites,
Just Earthlings dreaming through their dewy nights.

You saw where we could not, and dared to go
Where we would be destroyed; you showed
A kind of metal courage, and faithfulness.
Your cryptic, ciphered, graven messages
Are for ourselves, designed to boomerang

Back like a prayer from where the angels sang,
That shining ancient blank encirclement.
Your voyage now outsoars mundane intent
And joins blind matter's motions. *Au revoir*,
You rickety free-falling man-made star!
Machines, like songs, belong to all. A man
Aloft is Russian or American,
But you aloft were simply sent by Man
At large.   Sincerely yours,
                              A fan.

A Few Notes on the Poems

"Ode for Orville and Wilbur Wright"

bitter and . . . young: Wilbur Wright was only forty-five when he died of typhoid fever in 1912. Orville lived to be seventy-seven; however, he spent his entire life fighting to have the brothers' achievement properly recognized. Finally, in December 1948, the *Flyer* was installed in the Smithsonian—but Orville had died eleven months earlier.

"To Beachey, 1912"

Lincoln Beachey (1887–1915) started out as a dirigible pilot in 1905 and learned to fly an airplane in 1910, quickly becoming the most celebrated and daring of the early exhibition aviators. The first American to fly an inside loop, he is credited with solving the problem of surviving a spin. In 1911 he flew under the International Bridge at Niagara Falls and in the same year set a world's altitude record of over two miles. His barnstorming feats included picking up a handkerchief from the ground with his wingtip, flying multiple loops, and climbing a mile, then diving straight down. While he was performing this vertical dive in front of 50,000 people at the San Francisco Panama Pacific Exposition, the wings tore off his monoplane, which crashed into the bay.

"The Coming of the First Aeroplanes"

Like the other phrases in these lines, "luxon wall" is an astronomical term; it is associated with the theory that one cannot travel faster than light. A quasar is the bright center of a far-off galaxy, considered to be among the most distant objects in the universe.

"Flight"

On May 20, 1937, Earhart left Oakland, California, flying a Lockheed Electra. She was headed east in an attempt to circumnavigate the earth at the equator. On July 2, beginning the last leg of this flight, she and her navigator, Fred Noonan, disappeared in the South Pacific while en route to Howard Island.

"Ascent"

A skilled flyer, Anne Morrow Lindbergh (1906–2001) accompanied her famed husband Charles on many of his flights. In *North to the Orient* (1935) and *Listen! The Wind* (1938), she describes their airborne life in beautiful prose. But "Ascent" is her only published poem to evoke the images of flight.

"The World Goes Black"

This poem is one of a series Shomer devoted to the life of Jacqueline Cochran (1910–1980), a gifted and flamboyant aviator who won races and set records throughout her forty-year flying career; she was the first woman to fly faster than the speed of sound.

"'A Lonely Impulse of Delight'–W. B. Yeats"

The poem's title is taken from "An Irish Airman Foresees His Death," one of the most beautiful of aviation poems. Written in 1919, when Yeats was nineteen years old, it celebrates the memory of his friend Major Robert Gregory, killed in World War I.

"High Flight"

John Magee joined the Royal Canadian Air Force in 1940. On December 11, 1941, he was killed in England in a midair collision with another Spitfire. Just a few days after the United States entered World War II, his parents sent this poem to the *New York Herald Tribune*, where it appeared on the front page, capturing the public imagination.

Michael Collins carried "High Flight" with him to the moon. Ronald Reagan read it at the memorial service for the *Challenger* crew. A veteran pilot, a man who would rather be accused of landing with his wheels up than of reading poetry, will often keep a dog-eared copy in his wallet. It is among the most famous of aviation poems.

"Imperial Airways"

During the 1920s, Imperial Airways' daily *Silver Wings* service from London to Paris offered its twenty passengers a full-course meal, served by a steward in a white coat. The trimotor Argosy took two hours and fifteen minutes to cover the 220 miles between Croydon and Le Bourget airports.

"Flying"

This sonnet is one of the first poems to describe the experience of flying at night.

"The Unconquered Air"

These poems, one written before, the other after the Wrights' epochal flight, are among the earliest American responses to aviation.

"Dulles Airport"

Saarinen: Eero Saarinen (1910–1961), Finnish-born architect who designed Dulles Airport (completed 1962).

"Eagle Youth"

This is one of the very few American poems to describe aerial conflict in World War I.

"About Eyes"

The poem reflects Rolfe's experience in the Spanish Civil War as a volunteer in the International Brigades.

"The Death of the Ball Turret Gunner"

In both the B-17 and the B-24 bombers, the ball turret protruded from the belly of the plane. A small plexiglass sphere, it held two .50-caliber machine-guns. The whole turret revolved as the gunner, hunched over his guns, took aim at fighter aircraft attacking from below. He was, of course, exceedingly vulnerable to enemy fire.

"Tuskegee Airfield"

Prior to 1940, African Americans were barred from flying for the U.S. military. But in World War II a total of 992 black pilots trained at Tuskegee, and 450 were sent overseas. Flying first as the 99th Fighter Squadron and later as the 332nd Fighter Group, they scored 111 air victories, destroyed more than 250 enemy aircraft, and won over 850 medals. Sixty-six Tuskegee airmen were killed in action during the war.

"Cobra Pilot"

Cobra: the Bell Huey Cobra helicopter, an attack gunship flown in Vietnam beginning in 1967.

"Sonnet for an SR-71"

SR-71: strategic reconnaissance aircraft. Better known as the Lockheed Blackbird, this plane is capable of surveying the ground from 80,000 feet at a speed of Mach 3. It carries a multitude of highly sophisticated sensors—photographic, infrared, and electronic.

"The Lost Pilot"

Tate's father, a World War II pilot, was reported missing over Germany in 1943, the year the poet was born.

"Black Box"

"We're going down . . .": the last words uttered by the crew of Air Florida #90, seconds before it crashed into a bridge over the Potomac River. The plane had just taken off from Washington National Airport on that snowy afternoon in January 1982; seventy-four of the seventy-nine people aboard were killed, along with four others on the ground.

"Libyan Airliner/Egyptian Acrobats/Israeli Air Circus"

In February 1973, a Libyan airliner strayed off course over the Sinai Desert. The Boeing 727 was shot down by Israeli Air Force fighters; all 106 aboard were killed.

"Lockerbie" and "The Women of Lockerbie"

On December 21, 1988, Pan Am #103, a Boeing 747 overflying Locker- bie, Scotland, crashed after a bomb on board exploded. All 259 aboard were killed, as well as eleven local residents, who died in the fire that followed the crash.

"Above the City"

On July 28, 1945, a U.S. Army Air Forces B-25 bomber crashed into the Empire State Building, smashing a twenty-foot hole and setting two floors afire. All three aboard the plane were killed, as well as eleven others. The pilot had become disoriented in heavy fog while trying to land at Newark.

The last two stanzas include revisions in phrasing suggested to the young Laughlin by noted poet Marianne Moore.

"Dawn of the Space Age"

The chimpanzee Ham was launched on January 31, 1961, in a *Mercury* capsule; the success of his suborbital flight led to the launch three months later of Alan Shepard, the first American astronaut. Later that year another chimp named Enos circled the earth twice. His flight pre- pared the way for John Glenn, who on February 20, 1962, became the first American to orbit the earth, circling the globe three times.

"Ode to the Moon's Far Side"

Collins first rode into space in 1966 aboard the *Gemini 10* spacecraft; he and John Young orbited the earth forty-six times. Three years later

Apollo 11 took off on its historic mission. On July 20, 1969, Neil Armstrong and Buzz Aldrin landed the lunar module on the Sea of Tranquility while Collins, pilot of the command module, orbited overhead.

"Dog Asleep"

Laika: "barker" in Russian. A mongrel from the streets of Moscow, Laika was the first animal to go into orbit, but it was a one-way trip. Launched aboard *Sputnik 2* on November 3, 1957, she lived for several days until the batteries of her life support system ran down. Her satellite orbited for another six months before it slipped back into the atmosphere and burned.

"Heel & Toe to the End"

On April 12, 1961, Yuri Alekseyevich Gagarin became the first human to leave earth and enter space, making a one-orbit flight aboard the *Vostok I*.

"The Crew of *Apollo 8*"

On December 21, 1968, *Apollo 8* shot upwards on a flight that four days later took it into lunar orbit. Its crew—Frank Borman, James Lovell, and William Anders—were the first humans to escape the pull of earth's gravity.

"The Flight of Apollo"

Kunitz wrote this poem before *Apollo 11* was launched. "When I saw the landing on TV, I felt I had already been there. There was no need to change a word."

"*EVA* Psalm"

EVA: extra-vehicular activities, better known as space walks.

"Astronauts"

Taurus Littrow: region of the lunar mountains explored by Gene Cernan and Jack Schmitt of the *Apollo 17* flight (December 1972). They were the last astronauts to set foot on the moon.

"Elegy for *Challenger*"

On January 28, 1986, only seventy-three seconds after launch, the space shuttle *Challenger* exploded. All seven crew members were killed, including civilian teacher Sharon Christa McAuliffe. The cause of the tragedy was later traced to faulty O-rings in the solid-fuel rocket boosters of the shuttle.

"Viking"

Viking I, launched in August 1975, reached Mars eleven months later. On July 20, 1976, its lander touched down on the Martian surface. The orbiting probe continued to transmit information for another four years.

"Firmament on High"

Heimisch: homey. Eocene forms: beings arising, as did the mammals, in the ancient Eocene epoch.

"An Open Letter to *Voyager II*"

Voyager II was launched on August 20, 1977, and was designed to last only five years. The small spacecraft reached Jupiter in July 1979. Two years later it flew past Saturn, then Uranus (1986) and Neptune (1989), sending back detailed photos and other data on all four planets. Still operational, both it and *Voyager I* have since sailed on, out of our solar system and into interstellar space.

America in Flight

A Brief History

Any history of aviation begins, inevitably, with a litany of numbers. On December 17, 1903, the Wright brothers' *Flyer* skimmed the sand dunes of Kitty Hawk for 120 feet, skidding to a stop after twelve seconds. Later the same day their flimsy motor kite managed to fly almost half a mile in fifty-nine seconds. In the years and decades to come, the records for altitude, speed, and range continued this exponential growth. By 1909 the Wrights had developed an 80-mph racing model and, for the U.S. Army, a two-seater version with a range of 125 miles. A year later, competing pilots raised the altitude record to almost 10,000 feet, while the Wrights' main competitor, Glenn Curtiss, flying from Albany to New York City, stayed aloft for 2 1/2 hours. In 1911, Cal Rodgers flew coast to coast in forty-nine days. Ten years later Jimmy Doolittle made the trip in less than a day; in 2005 airliners cover the distance in fewer than six hours.

In Europe, where France soon took the lead in developing aviation, there were many other record-breaking events in the first decade of flight, including, in 1909, Blériot's crossing of the English Channel and in the same year a week-long air meet at Rheims that drew over 200,000 spectators.

While breaking records, flyers on both sides of the Atlantic were also inventing new maneuvers—loops, rolls, dives, and spins—but they were courting death in the process. In the United States Lincoln Beachey and Harriet Quimby were just two of the many pioneers who died when their fragile craft broke apart or exploded or simply crashed into ground or sea. With accidents so common, early aviation gained renown, not as a promising mode of transport, but as a curiosity, a sport practiced only by a small band of daredevils for the titillation of thrill-seeking crowds.

The military potential of aviation was another matter. In 1911, testing its new machines, the U.S. Army used a plane to drop a live bomb onto the California countryside. In the same year, Italian flyers rained grenades on Ottoman troops in North Africa. And in the course of the Great War,

Germany used first Zeppelin airships and later Gotha bomber aircraft to drop over 5,000 bombs on England, killing more than 1,400 people on the ground.

Though introducing a wholly new form of terror, these early experiments in aerial bombing proved ineffective and costly. And despite the high pro-file of aerial dogfights and the public's adulation of the aces, air power was not decisive in winning the war. Planes were valuable primarily for map-ping, reconnaissance, and photography of troop positions.

The United States, of course, did not enter the war until 1917; at that time the American army owned only about 110 planes, many already obso-lete. But nascent manufacturing companies like Curtiss and Boeing were soon contracting to build thousands of airplanes, flying boats, and aircraft engines. Meanwhile, the armed forces embarked on a massive program to train flight personnel, with 190,000 in uniform by war's end.

Both planes and pilots arrived in Europe too late to see much action on the battlefield. In fact, for American aviation the real effect of the war was seen after the peace treaties were signed. In an isolationist climate, the army and navy were soon selling off their glut of planes and Liberty engines. Many were snapped up by ex-military pilots eager to exploit their new skills. Others were acquired by women pioneers of flight, like Amelia Earhart and Bessie Coleman. Some of these flyers became barnstormers, touring the country offering five-minute joyrides (twenty-five dollars for a loop and a spin). Other pilots turned their planes to new uses: crop dust-ing, aerial photography, or stunt flying for Hollywood movies like *The Great Air Robbery* (1919), the Academy Award–winning *Wings* (1927), and Howard Hughes's *Hell's Angels* (1930).

But in the early 1920s the most important aviation event in the United States was the establishment of the airmail service. A government initiative begun in 1918, the first flights delivered mail between New York City and Washington, D.C., but the routes soon expanded westward to Chicago, then to Omaha and San Francisco. Besides employing a small army of pilots and planes, the airmail service dictated the construction of airfields all along its routes, plus a network of radio beams and lighted airways (18,000 miles of them by 1933). This infrastructure in turn facilitated the growth of com-mercial companies such as United Airlines.

Meanwhile, with aeronautics no longer just a novel diversion but a fast-growing industry, improvements in aircraft design developed at a furious pace: bigger and more reliable engines, variable-pitch propellers, retractable landing gear. To meet the demand for all-weather and night flying, engineers were spurred to design sleek, metal-skinned monoplanes, whose closed cockpits sported two-way radios, improved altimeters, turn-and-bank indicators, and other navigational instruments.

A succession of record-breaking flights made headlines throughout the 1920s and '30s. But it was one event in 1927 that electrified the public imagination: Charles Lindbergh's flight from New York to Paris. Lindbergh was not the first aviator to cross the Atlantic; that had been done six years earlier. But he was the first to make the flight solo and at a single go. And his grueling 33 1/2-hour journey dramatically linked two major capitals of the Western world. In the months following his flight, Lindbergh, an authentic hero and the darling of the media, toured the country to promote aviation. The success of his cause can be seen again in the numbers: in 1926 American companies produced a total of 650 planes; in 1928, 3,000 aircraft. The Boeing Company was joined by new corporations destined to become major players in aviation: Douglas, Lockheed, and Northrop; Beechcraft, Piper, and Cessna. As Joseph J. Corn observes in *The Winged Gospel,* "by the latter half of the twenties, the airplane had emerged as a practical and reliable means of transporting people and goods over great distances" (73). New American airlines like Pan American and TWA, having carried 6,000 passengers in 1926, were selling 3,000,000 tickets a year by the end of the 1930s. By then the DC-3, with its heated, soundproofed cabins and cruise speeds approaching 200 mph, had made long-distance flying fast and comfortable, while the pressurized cabin of the new Boeing 307 allowed a smooth, quiet flight above thunderclouds and snowstorms. In 1938 Pan American inaugurated a transatlantic service, using its glamorous 74-seat flying boat, the Boeing 314.

Then came the attack on Pearl Harbor. Once again airplanes were enlisted as weapons of war, this time with devastating effect. As in World War I, America was a latecomer to the conflict; in 1941 its air fleet lagged behind those of the European powers and of Japan in both numbers and technology. But airplane manufacturers and airlines were quickly drafted into the war effort. Over the next four years, the United States produced 300,000 aircraft, including B-17 and B-24 bombers, C-47 transports, and an array of grimly named fighters: the Lightning, Thunderbolt, Corsair, and Wildcat. In the Pacific theater, naval air power played a vital role in the battles of the Coral Sea, Midway, and Guadalcanal; in North Africa, in Italy, and in the Normandy invasion, pilots of the U.S. Army Air Forces helped assure Allied victory.

Even before the outbreak of global conflict, the Spanish Civil War had demonstrated the horrifying possibilities of precision aerial bombing—of airfields and factories, of railroads and bridges, and now of cities themselves. In 1939, President Roosevelt roundly condemned the bombing of civilians in Spain, yet in Seattle the mass production of the B-17 bomber had already begun. The fates of Madrid, Barcelona, and Guernica prefigured the dev-astation later wreaked on Britain (almost 300,000 casualties), the Allied destruction of Dresden (135,000 civilian deaths), the incendiary bombing of Tokyo by American forces (just one of the ten raids killed over 83,000 people), and finally the nuclear firestorms that leveled Hiroshima (78,000 dead, 13,000 missing) and Nagasaki (almost 74,000 dead). The success of this harrowing use of air power transformed the way future wars would be conceived and fought. In fact, ever since the creation of the U.S. Strategic Air Command (SAC) in 1946, the threat of nuclear attack carried out by intercontinental bombers has become a permanent factor in global politics.

When peace returned, civil aviation was poised to thrive. American airlines, building on wartime advances in technology and on their new expertise in long-range operations, avidly pursued opportunities in both domestic and global markets. Just a few months after the end of the war in Europe, transatlantic passenger service resumed, now using DC-4 land-planes equipped with radar. In 1948, Idlewild (later renamed Kennedy) Airport began operations, the first facility specially designed for aerial mass transport. The 1950s saw further expansion of the domestic aviation in-frastructure, while propliners like the Convair and the Constellation made flying a pleasure. Comfortable, reliable, fuel-efficient, they attracted an ever growing clientele, edging out first trains, then ships as Americans' pre-ferred option for long-range travel.

Then in 1958, the Boeing 707 began service. With its four jet engines, it could halve flight times while carrying as many as 180 passengers; and it was soon followed by the equally successful 727, DC-9, and 737, designed for shorter routes. The jet age had begun. In the late 1960s the development of turbofan engines brought even greater thrust and better fuel efficiency, which translated into longer range, lower fares, and larger airplanes (the Boeing 747, introduced in 1969, can carry over 400 passengers). Abetted by these advances, the 1960s saw a huge surge in air travel: in 1958, TWA logged 4.6 billion passenger miles on its long-haul routes, while in 1969 it posted 19.1 billion.

For the rest of the century, civil aviation continued to expand, with dramatic economic and social effects. By 1970 almost half of all American adults had flown on a scheduled airliner, many of them en route to a vacation spot. Entrepreneurs worldwide recognized that just by building an airport, any picturesque town or sleepy island might develop into a major tourist destination. Businesses could show off their success by acquiring a Learjet, rock stars by flying to Europe on the Concorde. The development of air cargo services meant that New Yorkers could buy freshly cut Thai orchids or start their day with a grapefruit grown in Cyprus. Laker Airways, People Express, and later Easyjet showed that low-fare, no-frills flight operations could attract plenty of customers. The airlines' adoption of hub-and-spoke routing allowed them to reduce fares as well.

By the 1990s GPS navigation, fly-by-wire controls, and computerized "glass cockpits" had vastly improved flight operations, while on the ground the advent of Internet booking and electronic ticketing offered greater flexibility to passengers. Although the deregulation of the 1970s and increased competition brought the demise of several big players, including Pan Am and Braniff, airlines in the United States at the end of the century were carrying over 620 million passengers a year, with 7,000 flights a day in and out of New York City alone. In 2000, Airbus Industries began production of a new super-airliner, the A-380, with a capacity of 550 passengers. Boeing countered with plans for its "Sonic Cruiser," designed to fly at nearly the speed of sound. The next logical step would be hypersonic flight; and even in the early 1990s U.S. designers were already developing the concept of such an "aerospace plane," capable of reaching a destination anywhere on the planet within four hours. An aeronautical engineering text published in 1999 could predict, with some confidence, "unlimited progress and opportunities in the enhancement of airplane performance and design in the twenty-first century" (Anderson 48–49).

In addition to advances in large-scale commercial flight, the latter half of the twentieth century saw innovations in sport aviation. Designer Burt Rutan pioneered the development of unconventional kitplanes like the *VariEze*. In 1986 his radically designed *Voyager* aircraft became the first plane to circle the globe without stopping or refueling. Its twenty-first-century successor, the *Global Flyer*, is designed to do the same—but in three days rather than nine and with only a single pilot. The popularity of gliders, hang gliders, and their mechanized cousins the ultralights has renewed the early appeal of flight as a sensory experience.

Long before the twentieth century began to wane, however, shadows loomed as well, darkening this rosy picture. Along with increased human mobility has come the spread of diseases such as AIDS and SARS, while aerial smuggling of narcotics, arms, and people has proved all too easy. Accidents, of course, have plagued aviation history since its very beginnings; and planes have always been exceptionally vulnerable to bad weather, mechanical failures, and human error. But with ever bigger aircraft and more crowded skies, the final quarter of the century set grim new records in accident fatalities, including the 583 people killed in the 1977 Tenerife collision between two jumbo jets.

An ominous prelude to future acts of terrorism, the first aerial hijacking occurred over China in 1948; prompted by personal or political motives or sometimes just plain greed, hijackings became commonplace, both in the United States (starting in 1961) and in Europe (which saw ninety-one incidents in 1969 alone). In recent decades airliners have been shot down from the sky—some accidentally, some with deadly intent. Other aircraft, like the Pan American 747 that exploded over Lockerbie, Scotland, in 1988, have been victims of bombs carried aboard. Worst of all—to date, at least—was the catastrophe of September 11, 2001, when four airliners were hijacked simultaneously, two of them flown into the World Trade Center, a third crashing into the Pentagon, the fourth plummeting into a Pennsylvania field. In some ways the century of flight that started at Kitty Hawk ended that day in New York City, when some 3,000 lives were lost.

Countermeasures, ranging from armed sky marshals to improved baggage and passenger scanning, have perhaps made airline travel safer, but also more burdensome and expensive. Before the events of September 11, 2001, airlines had confidently predicted a prolonged growth cycle. In the aftermath they have found themselves struggling to survive, as tourists elect to stay home and executives conduct their business through video-conference calls. In 2002, Boeing cancelled plans for its Sonic Cruiser, and a year later the Concorde flew its last flight. Despite these setbacks, aviation technology continues to advance. Ultra-long-haul airlines can now fly nonstop from Singapore to Los Angeles, a distance of over 10,000 miles. The Airbus A380, due to fly in 2006, will be capable of carrying more than 800 passengers. Gulfstream, the manufacturer of business jets, is at work on a supersonic model with a target speed of Mach 1.8. But economic and political downturns may yet ground these ambitious projects. Wars and terrorist acts, rising fuel prices, and faltering profits continue to dominate the headlines. By its nature especially vulnerable to such events, civil aviation faces an uncertain future in this opening decade of the century.

Military aviation, on the other hand, has taken a more predictable path in the last fifty-odd years. American air power played a significant role in the Korean War. At the beginning of the conflict, the air war was fought mainly by World War II vintage planes. But soon MiG-15s and F-86 Sabres were dueling in the sky over the Yalu River. The era of jet combat had arrived, its further chapters to be written in Vietnam, then Bosnia, the Persian Gulf, Afghanistan, and Iraq. Successive generations of U.S. attack aircraft (Intruders, Phantoms, and Crusaders; Tomcats, Falcons, and Eagles; Hornets, Nighthawks, and Raptors) fly ever faster and higher, carrying ever more deadly weapons. The second half of the twentieth century also saw the introduction of helicopter gunships, of high-flying reconnaissance planes like the U-2 and the SR-71 Blackbird, and most recently, of sophisticated unmanned aircraft like the Predator and the Global Hawk. In every conflict, aerial bombing has been central to U.S. military strategy, sustaining the production of huge long-range aircraft such as the B-29, the B-52, and the B-2 Stealth bomber.

Military imperatives were also the driving force behind America's space program. At the height of the Cold War, the Pentagon wanted missiles to counter the Soviets' ICBMs, and satellites to spy on Russian sites inaccessible to the U-2. Starting with V-2 rockets captured from Germany, both sides experimented with rocket propulsion. In 1947, U.S. Air Force major Chuck Yeager broke the sound barrier in a rocket-powered plane, the *Bell X-1*, and further experiments in rocketry continued throughout the 1950s. But when the Soviets' *Sputnik I* shot into orbit in October 1957, the space race assumed a new symbolic dimension, with the two superpowers framing their competition in terms of national pride and prestige.

For the next eight years, the Soviet Union maintained a strong lead in this race. The Russians were the first to launch an animal into space (Laika, the famous "space dog," in 1957) and the first to launch a man (Yuri Gagarin, who orbited earth for 108 minutes in April 1961). In May 1961, with great fanfare, the United States sent up Alan Shepard—but for only fifteen suborbital minutes; John Glenn's five-hour orbital flight did not take place until the following year. And although later that May President Kennedy committed the United States to a moon landing within the decade, the Soviets had already sent the unmanned *Luna 3* probe around the moon in 1959.

By the mid-1960s, however, the threefold American program was paying dividends: the Gemini series had put men into orbit; Mercury flights were perfecting techniques of living, working, and walking in space; and the Apollo missions were preparing for the moon landing itself. In December 1968, *Apollo 8* took its three-man crew into lunar orbit, their achievement broadcast live on television worldwide. This success led the Soviets to abandon their faltering lunar program; Russian scientists and engineers turned instead to the development of an orbiting space station.

On July 20, 1969, Neil Armstrong and Buzz Aldrin became the first humans to walk on the moon, bringing to fulfillment an age-old dream. Over the next three years, five subsequent Apollo flights continued to explore the lunar surface. By the time the last humans took off from the moon in 1972, they had collected over 800 pounds of moon rock plus enormous quantities of data—about the moon itself but also about the earth and the cosmos. The final Apollo mission in 1975 marked a significant shift in global politics: the American spacecraft linked in space with the Russian *Soyuz*, as astronauts and cosmonauts exchanged gestures of friendship.

Throughout these decades of space exploration, the United States has been sending satellites into orbit, many of them for military reconnaissance, but others dedicated to scientific or commercial uses: information the satellites have supplied on weather, crops, fisheries, mineral deposits, atmospheric pollution, and ozone depletion has proved immensely valuable. Satellite technology has also transformed air, sea, and ground navigation, as well as telecommunications, by relaying radio, television, and telephone signals worldwide.

At the same time, NASA has sent unmanned craft to explore the farther reaches of space. Probes like the *Viking*, *Voyager I* and *II*, and *Galileo* have vastly increased our knowledge of the planets Mars, Jupiter, Saturn, Uranus, and Neptune, while in 1983 *Pioneer 10* became the first human artifact to leave our solar system. In January 2004 two robotic probes landed on the Martian surface, transmitting close-up photos of its rock-strewn landscape. Later that year, however, came a major disappointment. NASA had sent the *Genesis* mission into deep space to collect particles of solar wind; but on its return, the capsule crashed into the Utah desert, destroying two years' worth of data.

And what of human space travel? In 1981 American astronauts returned to space, in the first flight of the Space Shuttle program. Over the next twenty-two years the shuttles would fly over one hundred missions, delivering satellites, conducting research, repairing the Hubble Space Telescope, and eventually helping to construct, operate, and staff the orbiting space stations—first the Russian *Mir* and then its successor, the International Space Station (ISS). Designed as a scientific laboratory, the ISS has experimented with the microgravity production of plants, metals, pharmaceuticals, and protein crystals—and has even hosted the first space tourists (at $20 million a ticket). In 2004 Burt Rutan's air-launched *SpaceShipOne* flew up to the edge of space, the first such rocket plane to be privately designed and developed.

But the operational cost of these ventures is high (each shuttle launch costing over $600 million), and tragedy has clouded their accomplishments. In 1986 came the explosion of the *Challenger* and in 2003 the fiery end of the *Columbia*. Before this latest catastrophe, optimists had predicted that humans would land on Mars as early as 2020, that we would soon establish a permanent base on the moon, that space would be the hottest tourist destination of the new century. But with a deficit economy looming and the American public still mourning the deaths of the seven *Columbia* astronauts, the future of manned space travel is in serious doubt. Will the new century see continued exploration and discovery, answering the calls made by politicians and scientists? Or will we retreat to the nearer horizons of our own blue planet?

Works Consulted

Anderson, John D., Jr. *Aircraft Performance and Design*. Boston: McGraw-Hill, 1999.

Beaver, Paul, ed. *The Encyclopedia of Aviation*. London: Octopus, 1986.

Bilstein, Roger. "The Airplane and the American Experience." *The Airplane in American Culture*. Ed. D. A. Pisano. Ann Arbor: U of Michigan P, 2003. 16–35.

Christy, Joe. *The Illustrated Handbook of Aviation and Aerospace Facts*. Blue Ridge Summit, PA: TAB, 1984.

Corn, Joseph J. *The Winged Gospel: America's Romance with Aviation, 1900–1950*. New York: Oxford UP, 1983.

Crouch, Tom D. "'The Surly Bonds of Earth': Images of the Landscape in the Work of Some Aviator/Authors, 1910–1969." Pisano 201–218.

Dickey, James. *Poems 1957–1967*. Middletown, CT: Wesleyan UP, 1967.

——. *Sorties*. New York: Doubleday, 1971.

Franklin, H. Bruce. "'Peace Is Our Profession': The Bombers Take Over." Pisano 333–356.

Goldstein, Laurence. "The Airplane and American Literature." Pisano 219–249.

——. *The Flying Machine and Modern Literature*. Bloomington: Indiana UP, 1986.

Grant, R. G., ed. *Flight: 100 Years of Aviation*. New York: DK, 2002.

Hedin, Robert, ed. *The Great Machines: Poems and Songs of the American Railroad*. Iowa City: U of Iowa P, 1996.

Pisano, Dominick A. "Bibliographic Essay." Pisano 389–397.

——. "The Greatest Show Not on Earth: The Confrontation between Utility and Entertainment in Aviation." Pisano 39–74.

——. "New Directions in the History of Aviation." Pisano 1–15.

Swenson, May. *To Mix with Time*. New York: Scribner, 1963.

Vas Dias, Robert, ed. *Inside Outer Space*. Garden City, NY: Anchor/Doubleday, 1970.

Weber, Ronald. *Seeing Earth: Literary Responses to Space Exploration*. Athens: Ohio UP, 1985.

Wohl, Robert. *A Passion for Wings: Aviation and the Western Imagination 1908–1918*. New Haven: Yale UP, 1994.

Acknowledgments

I am grateful to both authors and publishers for permission to reprint copyrighted poems.

"Climbing Out" from *Lady Faustus* by Diane Ackerman. Copyright © 1983 by Diane Ackerman. Reprinted by permission of the author.

"Elegy for *Challenger*" from *Jaguar of Sweet Laughter* by Diane Ackerman. Copyright © 1991 by Diane Ackerman. Reprinted by permission of the author and Random House, Inc.

"Flight" from *Navigable Waterways* by Pamela Alexander. Copyright © 1985 by Pamela Alexander. Reprinted by permission of the author and Yale University Press.

"Airplane" from *The Summer of Black Widows* by Sherman Alexie. Copyright © 1996 by Sherman Alexie. Reprinted by permission of Hanging Loose Press.

"The Coming of the First Aeroplanes" from *Ode to the Cold War: Poems New and Selected* by Dick Allen. Copyright © 1997 by Dick Allen. Reprinted by permission of the author and Sarabande Books, Inc.

"Flight Instructor" from *Lessons in Soaring* by James Applewhite. Copyright © 1989 by James Applewhite. Reprinted by permission of the author and Louisiana State University Press.

"A Leaf from a Log Book" from *Spanish Wings* by H. Babcock. Copyright © 1935 by H. Babcock.

"Eagle Youth" by Karle Wilson Baker. Originally published in *Yale Review* (1918).

"Over Ohio" from *Days We Would Rather Know* by Michael Blumenthal. Copyright © 1984 by Michael Blumenthal. Reprinted by permission of the author.

"An Aerial Photograph" by Thomas Carper. Copyright © 1984 by Thomas Carper. Originally appeared in *The American Scholar* (Autumn 1984). Reprinted by permission of the author.

"Dawn of the Space Age" and "V-J Day" from *Collected Poems*, by John Ciardi, ed. Edward M. Cifelli. Copyright © 1947 by John Ciardi, renewed 1997 by the Ciardi Family Publishing Trust. Reprinted by permission of the University of Arkansas Press.

"The Unconquered Air" from *The Unconquered Air and Other Poems* (1912) by Florence Earle Coates.

"Passengers" from *Picnic, Lightning* by Billy Collins. Copyright © 1998 by Billy Collins. Reprinted by permission of the author and the University of Pittsburgh Press.

Selection from "Ode to the Moon's Far Side" from *Carrying the Fire* by Michael

Collins. Copyright © 1974 by Michael Collins. Reprinted by permission of Farrar, Straus and Giroux, LLC.

Selection from "Cape Hatteras" from *Complete Poems of Hart Crane*, ed. Marc Simon. Copyright © 1933, 1958, 1966 by Liveright Publishing Corporation. Copyright © 1986 by Marc Simon. Reprinted by permission of Liveright Publishing Corporation.

"Earth's Bondman" from *The Ancient Bond* by Betty Page Dabney. Copyright © 1954 by Betty Page Dabney.

"Thunderbirds" by Tony Dater. Copyright © 1973 by Tony Dater. Originally appeared in *Listen. The War*, ed. Fred Kiley and Tony Dater.

"Sonnet for an SR-71" by P. L. Delano. Copyright © 1973 by P. L. Delano. Originally appeared in *Listen. The War*, ed. Fred Kiley and Tony Dater.

"The Flight" by Babette Deutsch. Copyright © 1927 by Babette Deutsch. Originally appeared in *The Spirit of St. Louis*, ed. Charles Vale.

"To the Moon, 1969" by Babette Deutsch. Copyright © 1969 by Babette Deutsch. Originally appeared in *Inside Outer Space*, ed. Robert Vas Dias.

Selection from "A Poet Witnesses a Bold Mission" by James Dickey. Copyright © 1968 by James Dickey. Originally appeared in *Life* (1 November 1968).

Selection from "Apollo" (Part II. The Moon Ground) from *The Whole Motion: Collected Poems 1945–1992* by James Dickey. Copyright © 1992 by James Dickey. Reprinted by permission of Wesleyan University Press.

"Vacation" by Rita Dove. Copyright © 1994 by Rita Dove. Originally appeared in *The New Yorker*, Condé Nast Publications, Inc. Reprinted by permission of the author.

"The Aeronauts" by Rhoda Hero Dunn. Originally appeared in *The Atlantic Monthly* (May 1909).

"On Hearing the Airlines Will Use a Psychological Profile to Catch Potential Skyjackers" from *New and Selected Poems 1974–1994* by Stephen Dunn. Copyright © 1994 by Stephen Dunn. Reprinted by permission of the author and W. W. Norton and Company, Inc.

"Courage" from *Last Flight* by Amelia Earhart. Copyright © 1937 by George P. Putnam, © 1965 by Margaret H. Lewis.

"The Fury of Aerial Bombardment" from *Collected Poems 1930–1986* by Richard Eberhart. Copyright © 1976 by Richard Eberhart. Reprinted by permission of the author and Oxford University Press, Inc.

Selection from "Wings" by Charles E. Edhold. Originally appeared in *Current Literature* (November 1909).

"The Crew of *Apollo 8*" by Elaine V. Emans. Appeared originally in *The Christian Science Monitor*. Copyright © 1969 by The Christian Science Publishing Society.

"The Raid" from *The Residual Years: Poems 1934–1948* by William Everson. Copyright © 1968 by William Everson. Reprinted by permission of Black Sparrow Books, an imprint of David R. Godine, Publisher, Inc.

John Wright. Copyright © 2003 by Robert Vas Dias. Reprinted by permission of the author and Permanent Press, in Association with Art First, London.

"'A Lonely Impulse of Delight'—W. B. Yeats" by David K. Vaughan. Copyright © 1973 by David K. Vaughan. Originally appeared in *Listen. The War*, ed. Fred Kiley and Tony Dater. Reprinted by permission of the author.

"FLT #4372" by Jeanne Murray Walker. Copyright © 2001 by the University of Nebraska Press. Originally appeared in *Prairie Schooner* (Fall 2001). Reprinted by permission of the author and the University of Nebraska Press.

"Tuskegee Airfield" from *The Homeplace* by Marilyn Nelson Waniek. Copyright © 1990 by Marilyn Nelson Waniek. Reprinted by permission of Louisiana State University Press.

Selection from "North" from *Departure: Poems* by Rosanna Warren. Copyright © 2002 by Rosanna Warren. Originally appeared in *Southwest Review* (2002). Reprinted by permission of the author and W. W. Norton and Company, Inc.

Selection from "Children of Adam" from *Leaves of Grass* (1863) by Walt Whitman.

"Heel & Toe to the End" and "Landscape with the Fall of Icarus" from *Collected Poems 1939–1962, Volume II* by William Carlos Williams. Copyright © 1953 by William Carlos Williams. Reprinted by permission of New Directions Publishing Corp. and Carcanet Press Ltd.

"An October Nocturne" from *The Selected Poems of Yvor Winters*, ed. R. L. Barth. Copyright © 1943, 1950, 1952, 1960, 1966 by Yvor Winters, © 1999 by Janet Lewis Winters. Reprinted by permission of Swallow Press/Ohio University Press, Athens, Ohio.

A project that spans twenty years incurs debts of many kinds. It is with deep gratitude that I acknowledge at least some of them here.

For their sage counsel on the selection of poems and the shape of the manuscript in its many drafts: Jane Chapman, Mary Olsen, Laurence Goldstein, Robert Hedin, Ann Jost, Rebecca Marsh, and the editors and staff of the University of Iowa Press.

For their invaluable help in locating poems and poets: Donald Anderson, William Ehrhart, Neil Farley, Jeremy Glover, Anne Goodyear, Phyllis Graham, Michael Harper, Christine Harris, Richard Heyhoe, Dan Jost, Jay Jost, Fred Kiley, Philip Levine, J. D. McClatchy, Deborah Ninios, David Olsen, Emily Rickert, Lee Saegesser, Denise Sokolowski, Deborah Stavrou, Michele Stepto, Robert Vas Dias.

For their generous staff assistance and excellent resources, the following libraries and institutions: George Washington University, the University of Maryland, the University of Minnesota, the public libraries of Portland, Oregon, and Rochester, Minnesota, the Library of Congress, the National Air and Space Museum, the National Postal Museum, Stanford University, the University of Toronto, Yale University, and the library systems of the U.S. Army, Navy, and Air Force.

For their invaluable support, academic and personal: my colleagues in the University of Maryland European Division, Athenian Ladies, Cretan Gentlemen, and other friends around the world, and as always, my splendid siblings Mary, Ann, and David.

I am especially indebted to Isabel Cabell, information manager par excellence, to Marla Lowenthal, amanuensis extraordinaire, and to Dori Kanellos, my own aviator-hero.

Index of Authors and Titles